NINE WAYS TO REACH GOD

A Prayer Sampler

Bridget Meehan, SSC, D.Min.

LIGUORI
PUBLICATIONS

One Liguori Drive
Liguori, Missouri 63057-9999
(314) 464-2500

Imprimi Potest:
William A. Nugent, C.SS.R.
Provincial, St. Louis Province
The Redemptorists

Imprimatur:
Monsignor Maurice F. Byrne
Vice Chancellor, Archdiocese of St. Louis
ISBN 0-89243-312-4
Library of Congress Catalog Card Number: 89-63838

Excerpts from *Daily Readings With St. Therese of Lisieux* and *Daily Readings From Prayers and Praises in the Celtic Tradition*, Templegate Publishers, Springfield, IL 62705, and are used with permission.

Scripture selections are taken from the NEW AMERICAN BIBLE WITH REVISED NEW TESTAMENT, copyright © 1986, by the Confraternity of Christian Doctrine, Washington, DC, and are used with permission. All rights reserved.

English translation of the Nicene Creed by the International Consultation on English Texts.

"i thank You God for most this amazing" is reprinted from XAIPE by E.E. Cummings, edited by George James Firmage, by permission of Liveright Publishing Corporation. Copyright 1950 by E.E. Cummings. Copyright © 1979, 1978, 1973 by Nancy T. Andrews. Copyright © 1979, 1973 by George James Firmage.

Excerpts from *Catherine of Siena: The Dialogue*, edited by Suzanne Noffke, copyright © 1980, and *Kything: The Art of Spiritual Presence* by Louis M. Savary and Patricia H. Berne, copyright © 1988, Paulist Press, Mahwah, NJ 07430, and are used with permission.

Cover art by Chris Sharp.
Interior art from *Eye Contact With God Through Pictures,* Sheed & Ward, Kansas City, MO 64141, copyright © 1986; *Proud Donkey of Schaerbeek* by Judith Stoughton, copyright © 1988; and Chris Sharp.

*I dedicate this book with love
and appreciation to my family
who taught me so much about God's love
through their love for me:
Mom and Dad, Aunt Molly, Patrick
and Val, Sean and Nancy.*

Contents

Acknowledgments   5

Introduction   6

1. Praying With Your Imagination   8

2. Praying With Scripture 17

3. Praying With Your Whole Being:
   Contemplative Presence 23

4. Praying With Another: The Art of Spiritual Presence 33

5. Praying With Art and Poetry 42

6. Praying With the Saints 55

7. Praying With Mary 78

8. Praying With the Church 96

9. Praying With Jesus 110

Suggested Reading 126

Acknowledgments

It is with profound gratitude that I thank my family and friends for their encouragement in writing this book. I am grateful to my parents, Jack and Bridie Meehan; my aunt, Molly McCarthy; my brothers and sisters-in-law, Sean and Nancy, Patrick and Valerie; and all the members of my family for their patient love and support throughout this process. I am deeply grateful to the many people who have shared with me their experiences of God's love through the years. I owe a special debt of gratitude to the following faithful companions who have taught, challenged, and supported me along the way. I thank Sister Regina Oliver, Sister Mary Emma Haddrick, Sister Michael Bochnowski, and the other Sisters in my religious community, the Society of the Sisters for the Church for their helpful advice and friendship; Irene Marshall, Peg Thompson, and Bob Schaaf for their generous service and loving care; Msgr. Charles McDonnell for his openness to dialogue; the Rev. Joseph Mulqueen for sharing this faith journey with me; the Rev. Francis L. Keefe for his constant encouragement; the Rev. John Weyand for initiating the Bread of Life Prayer Group; the Rev. Walter Montondon for his partnership in ministry; and all the members of the Fort Myer Chapel community for fostering my spiritual growth and understanding that different approaches to prayer can truly enrich our spiritual journey into the heights and depths of God's overwhelming love for us.

Introduction

Prayer is a journey in love. It is the recognition that we are profoundly, totally, boundlessly loved beyond our wildest hopes or dreams. It is the quiet listening to the whisper of divine love that can be heard in the depths of our being. It is the discovery of our profound beauty and tremendous worth as human persons. It is the affirmation that God is both companion and lover and that we are the beloved called to enter a relationship of intimacy and deep love.

This book invites you to experience God's boundless love by opening yourself to the infinite love of God revealed in different prayer paths. In my ministry as a pastoral associate I accompany individuals and groups on their spiritual journeys. I am aware that people today are searching for deeper relationships with God. I have come to the conclusion that an awareness of God's infinite love is the most important factor in growing in a personal relationship with God. This means that we need more than an intellectual understanding that God loves us as the gifted but limited human beings that we are. It means that we need to experience this love on a feeling level. Somewhere, somehow, in the depths of our hearts, in the marrow of our bones, we need to feel God's presence liberating, healing, and transforming us into new creations. We need to allow this profound intimate relationship with our God to shape and influence every aspect of our lives.

With *Nine Ways to Reach God* I hope to help you experience the power of God's love in your life in a new and deeper way. Each chapter begins with introductory remarks that present a specific prayer approach. After that you will find meditations or reflective exercises to help you explore that particular prayer path on your own. "Pray" this book in a leisurely manner, lingering over insights and feelings that seem to draw you closer to God. I have described briefly several methods of prayer. You may wish to try them in order or just skip around trying one that appeals to you, and if you find it unappealing in actual practice, move to another style until you find one that suits you.

At certain times in your life a different prayer path may be just what is needed to help you through a particular crisis or to help you experience God's love in a new way. Stay open and flexible. God may have some surprises in store for you.

One effective way of "trying on" a particular prayer style is to record your thoughts, feelings, and inner movements of the spirit in a journal. Tensions and anxieties can keep you from prayer. By allowing them to surface in writing, you can understand them, work with them, and bring them to God, asking for compassion and healing. Journaling affirms and deepens the experiences of inner life. The symbols that emerge during prayer times, the dreams you have, the deep emotions that you discover in yourself, reflect the unique person you are and have a significant role to play in your spiritual growth.

Nine Ways to Reach God is also written for group use. For group use participants could share insights over one or more of the prayer styles or choose one for prayer and/or discussion. For prayer you might read aloud one day's reflection and then try to listen together to what God is saying. For discussion you might want to relate the reflection to human situations in the family, at school, on the job, in a specific relationship, or share thoughts, feelings, or insights that touched you.

This book could provide opportunities for spiritual growth during Advent, Lent, or on a personal retreat. It could be utilized as a follow-up to Renew, De Sales, or any program for renewal or prayer. Charismatics, Cursillo participants, Marriage Encounter groups, single adults, single-parent groups, and alcohol- and drug-recovery programs could find it to be a helpful tool in spiritual development. The possibilities for this book's adaptation to individual and group needs are endless.

CHAPTER ONE

◆

PRAYING
With Your Imagination

Contemporary Christians are rediscovering the significance of the imagination in giving their prayer new vitality and life. Classic writers such as Saints Teresa of Avila, Ignatius of Loyola, and Blessed Julian of Norwich recognized the power of imagination and incorporated it into their own prayer lives. Each of these holy women and men knew that the heart of prayer is living in God's presence and knowing how to use their imaginations in this encounter.

Teresa of Avila described the stages of growth in prayer as a progression from lower mansions to higher mansions in a book called *Interior Castle*. This image came from her background as a sixteenth-century Spanish noblewoman who later became a famous reformer of the Carmelite Order.

Ignatius of Loyola taught a method of prayer that invited the individual to enter a biblical scene using all of the senses so that one became an actual participant in the scene.

In her book *Revelations of Divine Love* Julian of Norwich, a fourteenth-century English mystic, describes the Trinity in Jesus on the Cross. She focuses on the image of the garland on Christ's head, writing, "Great drops of blood rolled down from the garland like pellets, seemingly from the veins; and they came down a brownish red colour, and as they spread out they become bright red, and when they reached the eyebrows they vanished...."

Thus, praying with the imagination has a long history in Christian tradition, and as a contemplative path to prayer it helps people encounter God's presence in the ordinary in new and vital ways.

IMAGING PRAYER AND HEALING

Praying with the imagination can have an important healing effect on your mind, body, and spirit. You can use your imagination in prayer to get in touch with deep-rooted negative feelings such as anger, hurt, resentment, and hatred. As you share those feelings with God and experience God's acceptance of them, you allow yourself to get more in touch with those emotions. This enables you to feel free to express more painful emotions to God, to accept yourself with your hurt feelings, and to open yourself to the liberating, healing power of God's love present in everyday life.

Scientists and researchers confirm the significant role the imagination plays in the healing of people's bodies and psyches. Pain control centers in LaCrosse, Wisconsin, and at the University of California at Los Angeles are investigating new directions in the treatment of stress-related illnesses. Patients report to these centers with pain from back injuries or migraine headaches that medicine fails to relieve. By utilizing a combination of relaxation, meditation, and imagination, Dr. Norman Shealy at the Wisconsin center found that over 70 percent of his patients had at least 50 percent improvement, and of those at least half reported from 90 to 100 percent improvement.

Imagination has an amazing therapeutic effect on both mind and emotions. At a hospital in Westhaven, Virginia, Dr. David Schultz reached some impressive conclusions as a result of an experiment he conducted with depressed patients. He separated the patients into two groups. He asked one group to utilize positive fantasies and daydreams such as picturing themselves in a beautiful nature scene or hearing compliments from a significant person who liked them. The other group was instructed to allow daydreams and fantasies to arise without trying to guide them in any particular direction. The patients who were directed to focus on people encouraging them and beautiful scenes demonstrated a significant improvement in their depression. Dr. Schultz used some of these same methods with people not suffering from depression and discovered that nature scenes and other healing images caused positive changes in moods. Likewise, many psychologists and counselors have found that the imagination has a powerful impact on both emotional and physical health. Therefore, it seems apparent that throughout the history of Christian tradition and contemporary science the use of imagination in prayer and in therapy has had a powerful healing effect on people's whole being. (For more information on prayer and healing see the books *Prayer That Heals Our Emotions* by Eddie Ensley and *The Healing Power of Prayer* by Bridget Meehan, SSC.)

Imaginative prayer helps people experience God's love in a more vibrant, real way. We need images to fill our inner being with creative and powerful messages of divine love. We need images to open us to the gentle touch of God in our lives. Images reveal the fullness of God's passionate, tender, forgiving, healing, transforming love. They invite us to give ourselves totally to God and to others in generous service. Images tell us who we are and who God is. They invite us on a journey to wholeness and holiness.

HOW TO USE THIS METHOD

1. Relax and let go of the distractions around you. Become centered by getting in touch with your breathing. As you breathe in, become aware of the coolness of the air flowing through your nostrils and filling your lungs. As you breathe out, release any anxiety, fear, or resentment that you are holding in.

2. Move to the center of your being. You can do this by imagining yourself slowly descending in an elevator. As you descend each floor you may wish to count the floors starting with 20. You can also do this in a similar way by imagining yourself walking down a mountain or diving into the depths of the ocean.

3. Once you have quieted yourself in one of these ways, read the reflection for the day you have selected. Read it slowly and with an attitude of great respect. As you follow the prayer suggestion, be aware of any images, thoughts, or feelings that come to mind. You may wish to record these in your prayer journal.

Day 1

I believe
that just as a fish is surrounded by the ocean
so we are immersed in God's infinite love.

Prayer Suggestion: In the stillness simply immerse yourself in God's love. Allow divine love to saturate your entire being. Bathe in that love. Allow any inner fears about being loved to dissipate. Open yourself to the fullness of this love. Be aware of any images that may come to you.

Day 2

Imagine that God is whispering the following passage to you.

My beloved, I love you with a boundless, strong, vibrant, tender, passionate, gentle, forgiving love. Before you were conceived I knew you. When you were born I whispered my words of love in the depths of your heart. In every moment of your life I have been present loving you. You are precious. You are loved beyond your greatest expectations! I hold you close to my heart.

Prayer Suggestion: Imagine yourself being held close to God's heart. Allow God to touch you deeply. Experience God removing from your heart any negative message or image of yourself as unworthy of love. Let God squeeze from your heart any pain, hurt, or resentment that may be present. Open yourself to the overwhelming love which flows from God's heart into your heart, filling you with new joy, peace, and strength. Linger in this embrace for as long as you feel comfortable. What did you learn about God's love from this embrace? Did you experience peace, comfort, healing? Did you come to experience God in a deeper way in this loving encounter?

Day 3

But now, thus says the LORD,
    who created you, O Jacob, and formed you, O Israel:
Fear not, for I have redeemed you;
    I have called you by name: you are mine.
When you pass through the water, I will be with you;
    in the rivers you shall not drown.
When you walk through fire, you shall not be burned;
    the flames shall not consume you.

(Isaiah 43:1-2)

Lord, I fear the cost of discipleship. You are such a demanding lover. You ask for the gift of my entire life. You call me to trust you no matter what happens. It is the "no matter" part that scares me, Lord. Help me discover your gracious, gentle presence right in the midst of the trials, tribulations, and disappointments of my daily existence.

Prayer Suggestion: Imagine that you are climbing to the top of a mountain. As you slowly walk up the steep incline, the bag that you carry on your back seems to get heavier and heavier. You are very tired. When you reach the summit, you collapse with exhaustion. A stranger carrying a heavy piece of wood on his back approaches you. The wood looks like a very rugged Cross. He comes over to you and asks if he can rest with you for a while. Suddenly you recognize the stranger as Christ. He looks at you with deep compassion and love. You spend time with him sharing the fears and anxieties you have carried up the mountain in your bag. Christ seems to understand the agony you have endured as a result of these fears. Then, gently, Christ invites you to take each fear out of the bag and place it on the Cross. As you slowly begin to place each anxiety, anger, hurt, shortcoming, and failure on the Cross, you begin to feel a new freedom and peace. You experience Christ's desire for your healing and wholeness. The depth of Christ's love for you overwhelms you. Notice your reactions to the Cross as a symbol of passionate, healing, divine love.

Day 4

Can a mother forget her infant,
> be without tenderness for the child of her womb?
Even should she forget,
> I will never forget you.

(Isaiah 49:15)

Prayer Suggestion: The beautiful imagery of the love of a mother for her child reminds us of God's faithfulness. God will never abandon us. Nothing can separate us from God's nurturing love, not even sin. Imagine yourself as a mother, even if you are a man. Begin with the moment of conception. Then reflect on your pregnancy and the birth of your baby. Imagine how you would feel as you held your infant in your arms for the first time. Now imagine God as a mother who is loving and nurturing you.

Day 5

I enjoy God loving me in and through this day!
In each personal encounter
I am growing in the fullness of divine love —
open to giving of myself totally
to the God-presence!

Prayer Suggestion: Become more aware of God's presence in the ordinary events of daily life. Offer another person love instead of criticism. Reflect on one ordinary situation in which you have found God's presence. It might be an event from daily life such as shopping, exercising, working, sleeping, driving, serving others, and so forth. The ordinary trials and joys of everyday relationships provide you with opportunities to discover new aspects of God's wondrous love.

Day 6

An Intimate Friend

An intimate friend
invites us to be at home with ourselves
and enter into union with another.

An intimate friend
helps us accept our own incompleteness
and shadow side by touching gently
the pain within our hearts.

An intimate friend
challenges us to
live out who we are called to be
and to seek new horizons
of service to others
in life's ordinary events.

An intimate friend
helps us experience the communion
God has called us to have with one another.

An intimate friend
is one of God's favorite channels
of healing love in our lives.

Thank you God for the gift of intimate friends.

Prayer Suggestion: Have you experienced God's love through an intimate friend? Reflect on the ways this friendship has been a source of spiritual growth in your life. When you think of an intimate friend in your life, what image comes to mind? What qualities are you most grateful for in this friend? Is there a symbol of your love you'd wish to share with this intimate friend?

Day 7

A Healing Prayer Experience

God dwells in the depths of your heart where you are most vulnerable. God waits there to love, heal, and transform you. It is there that God wishes to touch you most deeply. Invite God to come fully into one specific area of your life or being that needs healing with the prayer suggestion below.

Prayer Suggestion: Like a gentle ocean breeze caressing you on a summer's evening, allow the warmth of God's presence to permeate your being. As you become more aware of this presence, be sensitive to anything that is causing you pain, confusion, fear, anxiety, anger, or resentment.

Enter a dialogue with these feelings. Ask where they come from. What is their source? Invite God to be with you as you reflect on the unresolved painful areas that cause you to feel anxious, guilty, angry, resentful, depressed, compulsive, bound, or imprisoned.

God invites you to come just as you are with all your weaknesses, with all your hurtful feelings, into the healing embrace of forgiving love. Relaxing in the arms of this infinite lover, feel warmth and tenderness filling your entire being — liberating and transforming you. God's love feels like a fountain of living water flowing over you — cleansing you in body, mind, and spirit.

God pours the soothing oil of compassion on any inner wounds that remain from childhood experiences, especially in the area of sexuality, or any rejection suffered in the past or present.

God is setting you free; you are journeying toward wholeness; God is loving you infinitely, passionately, totally, and completely.

Celebrate this healing encounter in a special way.

CHAPTER TWO

♦

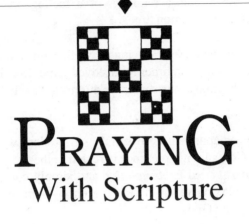

PRAYING
With Scripture

he symbols, stories, and images of Scripture give us many possibilities in prayer. Using imagination and visualizations can bring the Bible to life. As we begin to dialogue with and enter into symbols and pictures, we experience in Scripture ways for us to encounter God in a fuller and more personal way.

HOW TO USE THIS METHOD

1. One approach, called *meditation*, consists of reading a Scripture passage in such a way so as to allow the thoughts, feelings, and images to emerge spontaneously. One listens for some inner reaction, perhaps a thought or feeling or response, and pays attention to what attracts or repels.

In meditation one asks, "God what are you saying to me or what quality of your love are you revealing to me through this passage?" Perhaps a word or phrase will stand out. This can be repeated and used as a *mantra*. A mantra is a word or phrase that can be spoken or sung as an incantation or prayer. You can then use this mantra throughout the day as a reminder of a feeling or insight that occurred during meditation time.

2. Another suggestion worth trying is to reflect on or dialogue with the Scripture passage in order to discover some deeper insight or practical application to a particular relationship or situation in your life.

3. Still another approach is to simply sit in silent wonder, contemplating God's loving presence revealed in the Scriptures. This prayer form is called *contemplation* and simply consists of just "being" or relaxing in the divine presence — in total intimate communion with God.

If you want to try a combination of the three approaches you can read, listen, converse, make a practical application to daily life, and contemplate.

In the following Scripture reflections you may follow the suggestions provided after each passage or follow one of the above approaches. At times you might find it beneficial to return to your favorite passages, utilizing more than one of these suggested prayer forms.

Day 1

I will allure her;
   I will lead her into the desert
   and speak to her heart.

(Hosea 2:16)

Prayer Suggestion: Hear in this passage God's deep desire for a closer relationship with you. Encounter the divine lover of your life speaking within the depths of your being. What is God's presence like in the desert of your inner darkness and brokenness? What do you feel as you consider God speaking to your heart? Do you feel joy? Peace? Worry? Fear? Gratitude? Can you share these feelings with God? Listen for God's response.

Day 2

I drew them with human cords,
   with bands of love.

(Hosea 11:4)

Prayer Suggestion: Imagine the human cords of love — the bonds of love described in this passage. Imagine that these human cords join you with someone you love. Imagine these human cords joining you with someone who is difficult to love. What do you feel as you reflect on this image? Awe? Love? Fear? Anger? Gratitude? Share your feelings with God. Listen for God's response.

Day 3

I will espouse you to me forever...
   and you shall know the LORD.

(Hosea 2:21, 22)

God is intimately involved with you — loving you totally, boundlessly, passionately. The beautiful, faithful, generous love between spouses is the most beautiful symbol of God's love for humanity.

Prayer Suggestion: Imagine God as your lover. Is there a situation in your life in which you need God to embrace you? Is there a part of you that needs God's special tender love? Can you try to imagine God holding that part of you or that situation?

As you see, feel, and imagine that God is embracing you, what are your reactions? Do you sense love? Fear? Joy? Gratitude? Awe? Can you share these feelings with God? Listen for God's response.

Day 4

Can a mother forget her infant,
  be without tenderness for the child of her womb?
Even should she forget,
  I will never forget you.

(Isaiah 49:15)

As a mother's arms embrace her child, God's loving presence surrounds you. From the very beginning of life, God has tenderly shaped you — your body, mind, emotions, and spirit. God never stops thinking about you, longing for you, remembering you, loving you. You are special — one of a kind. In God's eyes, no one can take your place. You are unique and precious — the desire of God's heart.

Prayer Suggestion: Imagine God forming you in your mother's womb. Imagine God thinking about you, longing for you, remembering you, loving you. What are your reactions? Do you feel loved? Fear? Joy? Pain? Gratitude? Can you share these feelings with God? Listen for God's response.

Day 5

Though the mountains leave their place
  and the hills be shaken,
My love shall never leave you.

(Isaiah 54:10)

God's love will never leave you alone. Through all the tribulations and sufferings of your life, even the moments you feel deserted by family and friends, God's love envelops you. That love offers security and comfort. God's heart breaks for you when you hurt. God's love always offers you the courage needed to triumph over all negative and hurtful situations.

Prayer Suggestion: As you reflect on the Scripture passage on the previous page, what images, thoughts, and feelings do you experience? Do you feel fear? Gratitude? Love? Peace? Can you share these reactions with God? Listen for God's response.

Day 6

"While he was still a long way off, his father caught sight of him, and was filled with compassion. He ran to his son, embraced him and kissed him. His son said to him, 'Father, I have sinned against heaven and against you; I no longer deserve to be called your son.' But his father ordered his servants, 'Quickly bring the finest robe....' "

(Luke 15:20-22)

Jesus told this story to help us understand the compassionate love God feels for us in our sinfulness and weakness. Our failures should not depress us, but rather remind us of how wondrous God's forgiveness truly is. When we are a long way off, lost, alienated, wounded, and afraid, our God, who is like the loving father, runs out to meet us. In a way God indeed throws his arms around us, kisses us, clothes us with the finest robe of healing love, and invites us to celebrate our homecoming with our sisters and brothers in the Christian community.

Prayer Suggestion: Imagine God embracing you, kissing you, and clothing you with forgiveness and healing love. What thoughts and feelings do you experience? Joy? Unworthiness? Peace? Anxiety? Love? Can you share these feelings with God? Listen for God's response.

Day 7

My heart is overwhelmed.

(Hosea 11:8)

God wants you to experience the boundless love in the divine heart. God loves you infinitely, passionately, totally. Each of us is held close to all those we love in the divine heart. Indeed, all humanity is profoundly one in God's heart. This overwhelming mystery can fill you with wonder and awe.

Prayer Suggestion: Imagine God holding you in the divine heart. What thoughts and feelings do you experience? Awe? Joy? Love? Fear? Wonder? Now imagine God holding all humanity in the divine heart. What thoughts and feelings do you experience? Awe? Joy? Love? Fear? Wonder? Can you share these feelings with God? Listen for God's response.

CHAPTER THREE

◆

PRAYING
With Your Whole Being:
CONTEMPLATIVE PRESENCE

P rayer opens our whole being to the reality of God's tremendous love and makes us aware of this love working within us to bring human life to its full potential. When we pray, we develop a contemplative attitude toward all of life. Many people today feel a sense of alienation from the world and from one another.

Les Misérables, a musical about a young orphan, illustrates the loneliness that plagues contemporary life. While attempting to care for another, the lost orphan, Jean Valjean, struggles with his own alienation and loneliness.

In her book *Lost in the Land of Oz: Our Myths, Our Stories, and the Search for Identity and Community in American Life* Madonna Kolbenschlag proposes that the orphan archetype is "a metaphor for our deepest, most fundamental reality: experiences of attachment and abandonment, of expectation and deprivation, of loss and failure and of loneliness." Within all of us there is a spiritual orphan who yearns for the warmth of home. We need to befriend those parts of ourselves or those areas in our lives in which we feel fear, loss, failure, and loneliness. Only then can we allow God's boundless love to work there to bring us to wholeness and fullness. When we do this as individuals and a society, we can experience profound personal and social change.

One way of befriending the spiritual orphan within you and journeying toward a new unity with yourself, creation, other people, and God is by using the prayer of contemplative presence. This prayer can give you the opportunity to realize and to participate more fully in the ordinary and extraordinary happenings of life. It can help you discover God loving the "spiritual orphan" within you in all the events and relationships of daily life.

HOW TO USE THIS METHOD

The following contemplative prayer experiences invite you to involve your whole being — body, mind, and spirit. They provide you with different paths to enter more deeply into the creative processes of life and to discover your rootedness in and connection to the dynamic power of the Spirit's love present in the ordinary events of life.

1. Begin each prayer experience by quieting your mind and body. Become aware of how you feel physically. Take some deep breaths. Close your eyes. Be still and rest in God's loving embrace.

2. If you feel disconnected, anxious, or otherwise distracted in your prayer, embrace those feelings as "the spiritual orphan within." Then gently let them go.

3. As you become aware of your connection with creation, with others, with yourself, with all of life, and with God, you may wish to celebrate your oneness in some special way. You could take a walk; relax in a long hot bath; write a letter of reconciliation; go fishing, horseback riding, mountain climbing, swimming; create a song, poem, or dance; work on a painting, a piece of pottery, a needlecraft project; bake a favorite dish; listen to some favorite music; smile, laugh, and so forth. The possibilities are limitless.

Day 1

Know that I am with you; I will protect you wherever you go, and bring you back to this land. I will never leave you until I have done what I promised you.

(Genesis 28:15)

Prayer Suggestion: Take a walk in a park or wooded area. Imagine that God is at your side, holding your hand as you walk. Pause on your journey to smell the fresh scent of evergreen trees and wildflowers. Pick up a rock, acorn, leaf, or some other object of nature that attracts your attention. Examine the intricate design that nature has traced on it. Gaze on the beauty of blue sky and marvel at the cloud formations. Let your anxieties, fears, and frustrations float away on the clouds. Allow the warmth of the sun to caress your whole body. Feel the soft green grass and brown earth under your feet. Listen to the chirping musical score of the birds. Be aware of your connectedness with nature. You are one with all creation — with all of life. Enjoy the richness of God's splendid world. Absorb this awesome mystery — let it penetrate the core of your inner being. Allow it to embrace you, free you, nourish you, and fill you. Share the delight in your heart with God.

Day 2

And so I waited,
As we all have waited,
Knowing that we must have love
Even if there is no more of it in the world
Knowing that the solitary agony of Christ
Is the agony of us all at certain moments.
Waiting,
Waiting for the one
Whose Hand would be that of the Healer.

>(Anna Polcino and Eileen Horan in *Loneliness: Issues
>of Emotional Living in an Age of Stress for Clergy
>and Religious*, edited by James P. Madden.)

Prayer Suggestion: Imagine anything that is incomplete, for example, a camera without film, a kite without string, or a bowl with nothing in it. Begin by envisioning the incomplete object. Allow it to be a sign of your emptiness, neediness, loneliness. You may wish to write down your thoughts and feelings as you imagine the object.

Now become aware that God is present, loving you in the depths of your loneliness. Imagine the incomplete object you envision as now being filled. As you do so, try to simultaneously see it as a metaphor for how God is filling you with compassionate, tender love…surpassing your wildest expectations.

Day 3

They that hope in the LORD will renew their strength,
   they will soar as with eagles' wings;
They will run and not grow weary,
   walk and not grow faint.

(Isaiah 40:31)

As an eagle incites its nestlings forth
   by hovering over its brood,
So he spread his wings to receive them
   and bore them up on his pinions.

(Deuteronomy 32:11)

In Scripture the eagle is a symbol of strength, long life, and blessing. The eagle is an image of God who protects, carries, and nurtures us.

Prayer Suggestion: In this reflection, picture yourself as a young eagle learning to fly. Observe how your parent eagle carries you, supports you, encourages you to let go. How does it feel when you take the risk, venture out, and fly across the beautiful blue sky for the first time? Are you fearful? Excited? Joyful? As you continue your prayer, let go of all that holds you back from soaring like the eagle through the boundless love of God. Release fear, depression, resentments, anger. Open your heart as the young eagle opens its wings to receive God's strength.

During times of weariness, discouragement, and frustration, allow God to carry you on loving wings and to renew your energy. Let divine creative life flow through your entire being, filling you with new courage, enthusiasm, and joy. You are now ready to take new risks to proclaim the gospel in your life. You may wish to conclude this prayer by listening to, singing, humming, or even playing the song "On Eagle's Wings" by Michael Joncas.

Day 4

It is a beautiful experience
to journey within yourself
to the place
of deep peace and happiness,
the still point of your existence
and discover
love,
freedom,
empowerment,
God's presence.

Prayer Suggestion: Try the following type of contemplative prayer for at least 15 or 20 minutes a day. It will help you relax, let go of tension, and feel more energized for your daily tasks.

I let my body relax.
Relaxation is flowing through my head and my neck.
I relax my eyes
and my head
and my mouth.
I feel tension leaving the back of my neck
and my shoulders.
Relaxation is flowing down through my arms,
through my hands,
through my fingers.
My back and my chest are relaxing.
I feel the tension leaving my stomach,
my hips, and my pelvis.
Relaxation is flowing through my thighs
and my hips
and my knees.
My legs are feeling relaxed.
I feel the tension leaving my ankles,
my feet, my toes.
I now become aware of my breathing
as I inhale
and as I exhale.
I know that as I breathe in
I am breathing in the infinite boundless love of God.
As I breathe out
I am exhaling all negative thoughts and feelings.
I am breathing out anger
and hostility
and resentments.
I inhale
and I exhale....
The whole of my body and mind is relaxed and calm.
I dwell in God's presence deep within me.

Day 5

The world is charged with the grandeur of God. It will flame out, like shining from shook foil; it gathers to a greatness, like the ooze of oil....Because the Holy Ghost over the bent world broods with a breast and with ah! bright wings.

(Gerard Manley Hopkins in
Prayer That Heals Our Emotions by Eddie Ensley.)

Prayer Suggestion: When you are relaxed, calm, and centered in God's loving presence, imagine some of the most beautiful scenes from nature that you have seen — the warmth of the sun caressing your body on a lovely day, the diamond glitter of the stars at night, the red-golden sunrise splashed across the morning sky, the waters of the ocean crashing on the beach, the smell of a lush green meadow after a gentle rainfall, the fragrance of purple lilacs perfuming the spring air, the sound and sight of a violent thunderstorm flashing streaks of lightning across the summer sky, the pure white carpet of fresh snow covering the winter earth. Use your imagination and recall more scents, sounds, and sights. Remember the feelings they have evoked within you. Choose one of these memories. Open yourself fully to the beauty of this special moment. Allow the scene to express God's love for you in a new way. During times of loneliness and depression you may find it especially healing to prayerfully relive a favorite nature scene.

Day 6

The pain we feel for our world is living testimony to our interconnectedness with it. If we deny this pain, we become like blocked and atrophied neurons, deprived of life's flow and weakening the larger body in which we belong. If on the other hand, we let it move through us, we affirm our belonging; our collective awareness increases. We can open up to the pain of the world in confidence that it can neither shatter nor isolate us, we are not objects that can break. We are resilient patterns within a master plan.

(Joanna Macy, *Despair and Personal Power in the Nuclear Age.*)

Prayer Suggestion: Relax and be quiet. Imagine a beautiful gold or orange flame. This flame is the presence of God's love surrounding you. As you inhale, be conscious of God's peace filling you. As you exhale, let go of all anxieties, distractions, and resentments.

Now imagine people who are poor, homeless, abused, alienated, sick, imprisoned, and addicted. As these images of suffering come forward, be aware of humanity's tremendous suffering. Become one with the pain in the hearts of your sisters and brothers throughout the world and throughout history. Let the flame of God's light surround you and create in you a new solidarity with all those who suffer. Allow the warmth of divine love to fill your heart with compassion and a new desire to work for peace and justice. Observe the power of this flame spreading through all suffering people, destroying unjust structures that keep people oppressed, bringing peace among warring nations, and uniting all people in a new community — the kingdom of God.

Day 7

In the quote below, the unknown author of the book from which it comes is telling us how to approach contemplative prayer. In contemplative prayer we yearn for a deep love relationship with God. Our prayer begins when we become conscious of this longing deep within us. Sometimes this longing can be expressed in a sigh that involves our entire being. In this type of prayer we give our undivided attention to our beloved, entering into an intimate relationship with our God that involves our whole being.

> Lift up your heart to the Lord, with a gentle stirring of love desiring him for his own sake and not for his gifts. Center all your attention and desire on him and let this be the sole concern of your mind and heart. Do all in your power to forget everything else, keeping your thoughts and desires free from involvement with any of God's creatures or their affairs whether in general or in particular.
>
> *(The Cloud of Unknowing)*

Prayer Suggestion: Become relaxed and still. Be aware of your breathing. Inhale and exhale slowly, allowing God's love to breathe in you. Relax in God's embrace, and slowly read through the quote from *The Cloud of Unknowing.* As you do so, strive to follow the instructions the author has given to you.

CHAPTER FOUR

◆

PRAYING
With Another:
THE ART OF SPIRITUAL PRESENCE

One of the most beautiful occurrences in prayer is to experience the spiritual presence of another person. When we encounter the depths of another in prayer, we enter into the presence of God. This prayer form involves the creation of intimacy between persons. This is the prayer of heart speaking to heart.

Saint Gregory the Great described the impact of spiritual presence when he wrote, "Friendship is a union of souls and a joining of hearts." Gregory wrote to his friend Theotimus in the sixth century, "Friends are *cor unum et anima una* (one heart and one soul). As the love of God (caritas) is the custodian of virtue, so is my friend the custodian of my soul." (From *Kything: The Art of Spiritual Presence* by Louis M. Savary and Patricia H. Berne.)

Hence in loving another we discover the beauty of God's love within us joining our hearts in a spiritual communion. We become present to each other on a deep spirit-to-spirit level. In our relationships we learn to listen to each other and share with each other our ideas, feelings, and dreams. We can learn to experience the world and life through another human being's perspective. What does the person love? How does the person feel? What hopes and dreams does the person possess?

Praying with another person likewise involves entering into the thoughts, experiences, and feelings of the other. It involves loving the other as both gifted and broken in all his or her uniqueness. It gives us the opportunity to give and receive forgiveness, to experience healing and intimacy, and to encounter God's love radiantly alive in the depths of another's heart. Praying with another person helps us to experience the kind of profound spiritual union that Saint Gregory Nazianzen wrote about in a letter to his close friend, Saint Basil the Great: "It seems as though there were but one soul between us, having two bodies...you must believe this, that we are both in each one of us, and the one in the other...." (From *Kything: The Art of Spiritual Presence*.)

One way that we can experience this spirit-to-spirit connectedness with others is by initiating a prayerful dialogue with them. We can do this with people who are present and wish to participate in this encounter and with people who, because of separation or death or because of various obstacles or blockages, are not able to dialogue with us.

For example, let's suppose that your relationship with your brother is still influencing your life in a negative way. Maybe you cannot deal with the situation in real life because neither of you are capable of discussing the issues at hand because of old hurts or blockages that prevent any progress from happening. In your spiritual dialogue, however, you can open yourself up to him, move beyond your present obstacles, experience forgiveness and healing. The reconciliation that you experience from this powerful dialogue may indeed lead to the beginning of a new relationship.

Another way that you can experience the spiritual presence of another does not involve words but consists of simply focusing on the other in a contemplative gaze. As you lovingly look at the other, you can become joined to that other person in a profound spiritual communion. Words become unnecessary. You can experience a profound spiritual presence capable of energizing and strengthening both of you in life's greatest challenges.

Viktor Frankl, psychiatrist and author of *Man's Search for Meaning*, was a survivor of a World War II concentration camp. He credits his survival to the spiritual presence he maintained with his wife during his imprisonment. Here is a description of the spiritual communion that strengthened and sustained him throughout the darkest times of his life.

As my friend and I stumbled on for miles, slipping on icy spots, supporting each other time and time again, dragging one another up and onward, nothing was said but we both knew: Each of us was thinking of his wife. Occasionally I looked at the sky, where the stars were fading and the pink light of the morning was beginning to spread behind a dark bank of clouds. But my mind clung to my wife's image, imagining it with an uncanny acuteness. I heard her answering me, as with her smile and frank and encouraging look. Real or not, her look was then more luminous than the sun which was beginning to rise.

The following prayer experiences will give you an opportunity to "try on" both of these approaches to intimacy and spiritual union with another person. One day you may establish a loving union with a friend, spouse, parent, or child by simply picturing yourself standing face-to-face, smiling at each other. Even if you now cannot deal with the other, on another day there may be certain issues in a relationship that you *do* finally wish to deal with. Creating a prayerful dialogue at that time seems to be the best approach.

In the prayer experiences that follow, I have simply provided some possibilities to get you started. Both the prayer experiences and the steps listed below are, in fact, only suggestions to help you experience spiritual unity with significant people in your life. The key is to utilize what you find helpful and stay open to the Spirit's direction.

HOW TO USE THIS METHOD

1. Begin by quieting and centering yourself. You may find it helpful to get in a comfortable position and close your eyes.

2. Slowly take a few deep breaths. Simply pay attention to your breathing process. Be aware of the air passing through your nostrils as you breathe in and breathe out. Allow your body to relax.

3. Open yourself to God's presence in the depths of your own heart and in the heart of the other person.

4. Imagine his or her physical presence and hold the other in a contemplative gaze.

5. Become aware of your spiritual communion with the other person. You are one on the deep level of the spirit in God's presence. You may find it helpful to imagine the two of you joined together. For example, picture yourself and the person you wish to pray with walking hand in hand with Christ or surrounded by divine light.

6. If you wish and if it is appropriate, enter into a prayerful dialogue with the other person.

7. Share your thoughts, feelings, hurts, hopes, fears, and dreams with the other person. You can either do this verbally or in a journal.

8. Listen to the other person's thoughts, feelings, hopes, fears, and dreams, if you are able to actually communicate with this person.

9. Give and receive forgiveness for any hurts or disappointments experienced in the relationship.

10. Share the ways you experience God's presence in this relationship.

11. Observe any changes that occur in you and the other person as a result of this prayerful dialogue.

(The steps and examples described in this approach are adapted from the book *Kything: The Art of Spiritual Presence*.)

Day 1

Encounter With a Close Friend

Prayer Suggestion: Whom do you experience the deepest friendship with now? If the person is present, lovingly gaze on her or him. If the person is not present, form a picture of her or him in your imagination. Become aware of your spiritual oneness with that person. Share your personal feelings of gratitude and love for all this person means to you in a prayerful dialogue with that person and/or God.

Day 2

Your Most Challenging Relationship

Prayer Suggestion: Who is the one difficult person in your life who God wants you to love more? If the person is present, lovingly gaze on her or him. If the person is not present, form a picture of her or him in your imagination. Become aware of your spiritual oneness with that person. Begin a prayerful dialogue with that person and/or God.

Day 3

Dialogue With a Family Member

Prayer Suggestion: Select a member of your family with whom you wish to become joined lovingly in a spiritual communion. If the person is present, lovingly gaze on her or him. If the person is not present, form a picture of her or him in your imagination. Become aware of your spiritual oneness with that person. Begin a prayerful dialogue with that person and/or God.

Day 4

Dialogue With a Loved One Who Has Died

Praying for the deceased is an important way we can grieve their loss and focus on the loving union we have with them in God's presence.

Prayer Suggestion: Select a member of your family, a friend, or other significant person who has died and for whom you still grieve. Form a picture of him or her in your imagination. Begin a prayerful dialogue with that person. Do not be afraid of expressing feelings of grief, anger, or loss with this person. Now, forgive this person for leaving you. Spend whatever time you need giving and receiving forgiveness in this relationship. Surrender this person into God's loving embrace. Become aware of a deep spiritual oneness you have with the person. Allow God to fill any emptiness or loneliness you still experience.

Day 5

Dialogue With a Favorite Mentor, Teacher, or Leader

Prayer Suggestion: Who in your life has inspired you, encouraged you, affirmed your gifts, consoled you in your weakness? In what ways have you become more like this person?

If the person is present, lovingly gaze on him or her. If the person is not present, form a picture of him or her in your imagination. Become aware of your spiritual oneness with that person. Begin a prayerful dialogue. Share your feelings of gratitude with the person for all he or she did to affirm your talents. Now, share with this person ways in which you are growing more like him or her in your relationships with others.

Day 6

Dialogue With Mary, Mother of Jesus, or a Favorite Saint

Whenever we pray with Mary or the saints, we believe that they are spiritually present to us and are willing to intercede or share their spiritual gifts with us.

In *Kything: The Art of Spiritual Presence* the authors share some interesting results of this kind of prayer from their workshop experiences. "One woman asked from Peter the Apostle the gift of authenticity and spontaneity, which he gladly shared with her. Peter in turn wanted from her an ability...to listen sensitively. From both Teresa of Avila and Catherine of Siena another woman asked for wisdom in leadership. They in turn asked her to give them a sense of contemporary women in the Church."

Prayer Suggestion: Form a picture of Mary or a favorite saint in your imagination. Become aware of your spiritual oneness with that being. Begin a prayerful dialogue. Share with Mary or your favorite saint your thoughts, feelings, anxieties, fears, joys. If you need a special gift, ask for it. Feel free to offer to share a special gift you have with Mary or the saint.

Day 7

An Encounter With Christ

"I pray not only for them, but also for those who will believe in me through their word, so that they may all be one, as you, Father, are in me and I in you, that they also may be in us, that the world may believe that you sent me. And I have given them the glory you gave me, so that they may be one, as we are one, I in them and you in me, that they may be brought to perfection as one, that the world may know that you sent me, and that you loved them even as you loved me."

(John 17:20-23)

This passage about the indwelling among Jesus, the Father, and all believers stresses spiritual communion or oneness. Jesus tells us that because of our oneness with him we are energized to speak and act with his power. "If you remain in me and my words remain in you, ask for whatever you want and it will be done for you" (John 15:7).

Prayer Suggestion: Become aware of Jesus' presence. You may wish to imagine Jesus in one of the following ways: baby in the manger, itinerant preacher, healer, teacher, on the Cross, resurrected.

Become aware of your spiritual oneness with Jesus who dwells within you and in whom you dwell along with God, the Holy Spirit, and all believers. Your inner spirit is truly God's dwelling place.

Begin a prayerful dialogue. Share your thoughts, feelings, anxieties, joys, anger, and happiness with Jesus. Listen to Jesus' response to you. Realize that this dialogue with Jesus may go beyond words. You may feel Christ's presence by a sense of warmth in your hands as you pray or by experiencing the image of a certain symbol. Stay open to the Spirit's guidance as you pray.

CHAPTER FIVE

◆

PRAYING
With Art and Poetry

rtists, like poets, have a deep awareness of what is around them and inside of them. They take time to go below the surface of things and to contemplate life in its depths.

Christians are also called to grasp life in its mysterious beauty. Like the saints, poets, and artists, we desire to live life fully. Jesus tells us, "I came so that they might have life and have it more abundantly" (John 10:10).

Art and poetry provide us with two different approaches to living life in the depths and to encountering the Spirit of God loving us in those depths. Art and poetry encourage us to delight in the God we belong to and whom we encounter in the ordinary circumstances of each day, like driving to work, studying, preparing meals, and so forth. Art and poetry help us become more aware that God's presence permeates every aspect of existence and indeed fills the whole world. Art and poetry give us tools to contemplate and live life in its depths.

We are God's greatest works of art (see Ephesians 2:10). We are being created, healed, and transformed by Christ, who Vincent Van Gogh observed "is more of an artist than the artists who are working in living flesh and living spirit, made living people, instead of statues!" (From *The Complete Letters of Vincent Van Gogh*.)

Each of us, too, is an artist as we experience the profound love of God pulsing within and around us. In Morton T. Kelsey's book *The Other Side of Silence: A Guide to Christian Meditation*, he writes,

> Each of us becomes the artist as we allow ourselves to be open to the reality of the Other and give expression to that encounter either in words or pain or stone or in the fabric of our lives. Each of us who has come to know and relate to the Other and expresses this in any way is an artist in spite of himself/herself....In the final analysis meditation is the art of living life in its fullest and deepest. Genuine religion and art are two names for the same incredible meeting with reality and give expression to that experience in some manner.

Hence, we can say that people who experience God are artists and poets, and that art and poetry are mirrors through which we see God's boundless, passionate love permeating life.

The prayer experiences in this chapter use the medium of simple art forms such as illustrations and mandalas. *Mandala* is the Sanskrit word for "circle." Mandalas are often found in Oriental art, and they express the infinity and wonder found in spiritual realities like God. For more information on mandalas see *Coming Home: A Handbook for Exploring the Sanctuary Within* by Betsy Caprio and Thomas Hedberg.

A variety of poetic forms such as hymns and psalms can also provide you with different opportunities to reflect on the beauty of God's loving presence in the depths of life.

43

HOW TO USE THIS METHOD

The following suggestions can help you learn to use this prayer form.

1. Reflect on the poem or artistic illustration in a quiet and leisurely manner.

2. Allow a word, phrase, or image from the poem or illustration to touch you. If a word or phrase comes to mind, you may wish to repeat it as a *mantra*. A mantra is similar to what many Catholics remember as the short prayer phrases they were encouraged to repeat throughout the day to keep them mindful of God's presence; for example, "Sacred Heart of Jesus, I place my trust in you." Repeating a mantra such as "I belong to God" throughout the day may be a way of internalizing the message you have received from the poem or illustration in the day's meditation.

3. Another way of praying with art and poetry is to simply read the poem or look at the art and allow it to come to life within you. Live with it, dialogue with it. Ponder its meaning. Contemplate its richness. Let it fill you. Let yourself fill it. For example, while looking at a picture of a beautiful sunrise, you might invite it to move inside you. In doing this you could feel and act like the sunrise. Experience for yourself the immensity of God's love. Let that love spread its healing rays throughout your entire being like gold splashing across the morning sky, radiating hope for a new day.

4. Sketch, paint, sculpt, or write about any inner image that comes to you as a result of your reflection on poetry or art. Such activities can provide ways for you to befriend the inner life within you so that you may grow to appreciate more profoundly God's presence in the uncharted depths of your soul. Psychologists tell us that we human beings contain areas we are aware or "conscious" of and areas that lie deep within us which we are unaware or "unconscious" of. The aspects of our personhood that we are unaware of often get revealed to us through dreams, art, and painting — through so-called "right brain" language. One reason they are so important is because they utilize the preverbal language of pictures and symbols to put us in touch with our inner depths where God dwells and is constantly present for us.

In Scripture, God speaks both through the conscious and unconscious dimensions of the person. In both the Old and New Testaments there are numerous revelations of God's plan. Prophets like Jeremiah and Isaiah clearly taught God's Chosen People what it meant to be faithful to the God who was loving them with a covenantal love. In the Passion and Resurrection of Jesus Christ the depths of divine love are fully manifested. Christians throughout the ages have known, believed, and strived to live according to the example of Jesus Christ. When we give our mind, feelings, and will to the Good News of the gospel, this involves the giving of the self we know and are in control of — the conscious self — to God.

In the Scriptures we also discover that God reveals the divine plan through the unconscious — the self we do not know and are not in control of — in dreams.

Samuel, an Old Testament prophet, was called by God in a dream. "Then Eli understood that the LORD was calling the youth. So he said to Samuel, 'Go to sleep, and if you are called, reply, "Speak, LORD, for your servant is listening" ' " (1 Samuel 3:8-9).

When you utilize dreams, symbols, paintings, and other images in prayer, you open the unconscious self you do not know to the God hidden within the depths of your being. This can provide you with rich opportunities for spiritual growth. As you pursue this inner journey, it is helpful to have a spiritual director to befriend and assist you in the discernment process. A spiritual director can show you any blockages and opportunities for growth in the material that comes from the inner depths of your being. That will enable you to become a more whole and holy person.

Day 1

Can you recall a special dream or experience in which you felt God's love or protective presence? Try to live it again. Dialogue with it. Ponder its meaning. Contemplate its richness. Let it fill you.

Prayer Suggestion: Sketch or paint an inner image. Find a picture like it in a magazine or select a religious symbol that reminds you of this experience. Use this picture or religious symbol as a visual prayer to help you ponder more deeply the meaning of this experience.

In a breathing meditation, look at the picture or symbol. With each breath, take in its beauty, color, freedom, strength, healing power, love, and peace. With each exhalation, share its beauty, color, freedom, strength, healing power, love, peace with a significant person in your life, a group of people you are praying for, and/or the entire world.

Day 2

Praying With Art

Praying with art helps us transcend ourselves and deepen our awareness and vision of God's presence in life's depths. Let us rejoice in the beauty which we encounter in art.

Prayer Suggestion: Select a favorite painting or art object in your home or in a museum. Begin your prayer by taking a few deep breaths to relax your body. Become present to the art object or painting. Allow images to surface during your meditation. Be aware of thoughts and feelings that occur. Share these images, thoughts, and feelings with God. One way of doing this is to draw or write about these experiences in your prayer journal.

Day 3

i thank You God for most this amazing

i thank You God for most this amazing
day: for the leaping greenly spirits of trees
and a blue true dream of sky; and for everything
which is natural which is infinite which is yes

(i who have died am alive again today,
and this is the sun's birthday; this is the birth
day of life and of love and wings; and of the gay
great happening illimitably earth)

how should tasting touching hearing seeing
breathing any — lifted from the no
of all nothing — human merely being
doubt unimaginable You?

(now the ears of my ears awake and
now the eyes of my eyes are opened)

(E.E. Cummings, *Complete Poems 1913-1962*, Volume 2)

47

Prayer Suggestion: Select some classical or instrumental music to accompany your meditation on the poem on the previous page. Does this poem reflect the beauty of the Resurrection in a fresh way? What thoughts and feelings does it evoke in you?

Select an image, metaphor, word, or symbol from the poem that touches you on a spiritual level. Dialogue with it. Ponder its meaning. Contemplate its richness. Let it fill you. Use this word, phrase, or metaphor as a centering prayer or mantra. Repeat it during your prayer time and throughout the day to give you a deeper appreciation for the new life you share in the risen Christ.

Day 4

Praying With a Mandala

One way of exploring your love relationship with God and with significant others in your life is by designing your own mandala.

A mandala is a special drawing that is made of different shapes to reflect the dialogue between the visible and invisible, earth and heaven, matter and spirit, the conscious and unconscious. A mandala has two basic parts:

The *boundary* which can be made from several possible shapes. The edges of the boundary are equidistant from the center point, which may take a variety of shapes or which may be represented by some symbolic object or picture. Here are some examples.

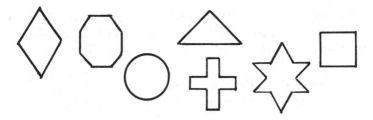

The *center* of the mandala represents God's presence within you. For this you could use a depiction of the sun, light, a tree, a waterfall, a flower, a star, a cross, a heart, or any other image of God you create yourself.

The space within the boundary is divided up. It might resemble a mansion, a wheel's spokes, branches of a tree, petals on a flower, rays from the sun, or streams of water flowing from a spring or fountain.

(For more information on this topic, see *Coming Home: A Handbook for Exploring the Sanctuary Within* by Betsy Caprio and Thomas M. Hedberg.)

Prayer Suggestion: Calm and center yourself. Reflect on the overwhelming love of God at the center of your being. Allow a picture to form in your imagination that expresses the depth of your love relationship with God and with others.

Draw or paint your mandala following the instructions on the previous page. You may wish to select classical or instrumental music that fits your reflection and use it for background prayer as you paint or draw your mandala.

The mandala can be used as a visual centering form of prayer. Gaze at the mandala. Breathe in the love, power, and beauty of God's love that radiates from the mandala. Let it fill you with harmony and peace. Breathe out this love, beauty, harmony, and peace to the whole world.

During times of stress, picture yourself at the center of the mandala in God's loving presence. Allow that love to saturate you and flow through you — liberating, healing, transforming, and energizing you.

Day 5

The Mustard Seed

He [Jesus] said, "To what shall we compare the kingdom of God, or what parable can we use for it? It is like a mustard seed that, when it is sown in the ground, is the smallest of all the seeds on the earth. But once it is sown, it springs up and becomes the largest of plants and puts forth large branches, so that the birds of the sky can dwell in its shade."

(Mark 4:30-32)

Prayer Suggestion:

Reflect on what Jesus meant by this parable, then reflect on the mustard seed as a symbol of your spiritual life.

What areas in your spiritual journey started out as seeds but in time became like the beautiful plant capable of providing nourishment and growth for others? Spend time praising and thanking God for these areas of growth.

What areas are still like small seeds that need nourishment to grow? Are there any obstacles that you need to remove in order to foster spiritual growth in these areas? Ask God to reveal these areas to you so that you can discern God's will in these matters. If sin or failure is involved, repent and pray for forgiveness and healing. Plan to participate in the sacrament of Reconciliation.

Select one area in your spiritual life that needs to be nourished. Develop a plan of action. Prayer, Scripture reading, celebration of the sacraments, fasting, almsgiving, or service to neighbor are some possible approaches that you can utilize. Share this plan with a spiritual guide or friend. Pray for the strength to follow through on your plan of action.

Day 6

Hymn of a Grateful Heart

I will give thanks to you, O LORD, with all my heart,
[for you have heard the words of my mouth;]
in the presence of the angels I will sing your praise....
Because of your kindness and your truth;
for you have made great above all things
your name and your promise.
When I called, you answered me;
you built up strength within me....
Though I walk amid distress, you preserve me;
against the anger of my enemies you raise your hand;
your right hand saves me.
The LORD will complete what he has done for me;
your kindness, O LORD, endures forever;
forsake not the work of your hands.

(Psalm 138:1-3,7-8)

Prayer Suggestion: Pray this psalm slowly with a spirit of love and thanksgiving for all the marvelous deeds God has done for you.

Reflect on the symbol of the heart. Ponder different ways that the heart reflects love and thanksgiving. How can you grow in a deeper spirit of love and thanksgiving in your prayer life?

Try to become more aware of the people you meet today. Look at people in your family, at work, in class, and on the street. Look on them with kindness and compassion. Hold them in your heart close to Christ.

Use the heart as a symbol for intercessory prayer. Place all the people and intentions that you wish to pray for in God's heart. Ask God to hold each one in the divine heart of love. Let go of all anxiety and concern. Be at peace. God is touching, healing, loving, providing for each need in ways that surpass your greatest expectations.

Ponder ways you can develop a steadfast heart. How can you grow in a deeper trust in and openness to God? From what fears do

you need God to save you? What distresses you? How can God liberate you?

If you suffer the distress of a poor self-image, be aware of yourself as a person God loves. Look at yourself each day with the loving perspective of your God who is always ready to forgive, heal, transform, and empower you. Then you will become more open to face the normal stress and challenges involved in daily living.

Day 7

Oh, only for so short a while you
have loaned us to each other,
because we take form in your act
of drawing us,
and we take life in your painting us,
and we breathe in your singing us.
But only so so short a while
have you loaned us to each other.

(Ancient Aztec Prayer)

Prayer Suggestion: If you see life and people as being on loan to you, you can see all as gifts. It is not good to cling tightly to relationships or to hoard earthly treasures. Revere all that you have with deep gratitude, and hold everything in open hands.

Reflect on the symbol of open hands. During your prayer time, open your hands and surrender all the important treasures and relationships of your life to God. Do you experience any obstacles in letting go and giving everyone and everything to God? Be aware of your feelings. Are you joyful? Anxious? Sad? Afraid? Share these feelings with God. Spend time expressing your gratitude to God for each gift and relationship.

What does the perspective of "all is on loan" say to you in your present relationships and in your present circumstances? Find concrete ways to express your love and gratitude to people you often take for granted.

CHAPTER SIX

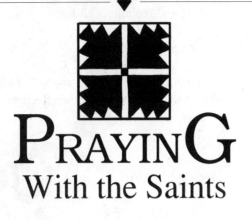

PRAYING
With the Saints

The Church has a beautiful tradition of raising up holy women and men as role models and guides on the journey to holiness. These holy people are referred to as saints because their lives provide us with examples of human beings who, in spite of their human weaknesses and failures, lived the Christian life with deep love.

In this chapter are the writings of seven different saints. They are people who were giants in their spiritual journeys and who provide us with inspiring reflections on God's love. For each day of the week there is a brief summary of the saint's life, a reflection written by that saint, and several prayer suggestions.

HOW TO USE THIS METHOD

1. Begin by reading a summary of the saint's life.

2. Pray a reflection from the saint's writings with your total being.

Use your imagination to picture poetic images. Be aware of any thoughts or feelings that are stirred as you pray.

3. Share these thoughts and feelings with Jesus.

4. Sit in silence savoring God's love.

5. Before concluding your prayer time ask yourself if there are any changes you need to make as a result of this reflection.

Day 1

Saint Therese of Lisieux

Therese Martin, the ninth child of Louis Martin and Zelie Guerin, was born in 1873 in the Normandy town of Alencon. Therese was brought up in a loving religious family. She was close to her mother, father, and sisters.

Therese contemplated spiritual realities at a very early age. Her mother's letters to Pauline, Therese's sister, refer to Therese asking and talking about heaven before she was three years old!

When her mother died, Therese was only four years old. At that time her personality changed; the formerly vivacious little girl became shy, timid, and sensitive.

Until age 13 Therese tended to be scrupulous and sensitive, easily breaking into tears at the least provocation. Therese dreamed of entering Carmel and sought admission at the age of 15. She encountered much opposition to this idea, even from the local bishop. Undaunted, she journeyed to Rome and approached Pope Leo XIII who told her she would enter "if it was God's will." She finally reached her goal and entered Carmel on April 9, 1888.

Therese spent the rest of her life living her "little way" of spiritual devotion in Carmel. At the request of her religious superior, Therese started writing her autobiography *The Story of a Soul,* in 1894. The book stressed the importance of paying attention to the small, everyday things in life. In it she wrote,

> For a long time my place of meditation was near a sister who fidgeted incessantly, either with her rosary or with something else. Possibly I alone heard her because of my very sensitive ear, but I cannot tell you to what extent I was tried by the irritating noise. There was a strong temptation to turn around and with one glance to silence the offender. Yet in my heart I knew I ought to bear with her patiently, for the love of God, first of all, and also to avoid causing her pain....So I tried to find pleasure in the disagreeable noise. Instead of vainly attempting not to hear it, I set myself to listen attentively as though it were delightful music, and my meditation — which was not the prayer of "quiet" — was passed in offering this music to the Lord. You see I am a very little soul and can offer God only very little things.

Therese suffered a long, painful death from tuberculosis and died at age 24. Pope Pius XI canonized her on May 17, 1925.

Prayer Suggestion: Read and pray the following reflection with Saint Therese.

Jesus Alone Is

Jesus alone is; the rest is not.
When in my youthful heart was kindled
The fire which we call love
You came then, Lord, to claim it;
And you alone O Jesus, could fill my soul;
For boundless was the need I felt of loving you.

To be with you and in you is my one and only desire.

Let us be one with Jesus…let us make our
life a continual sacrifice, a martyrdom of love to
console Jesus. May all moments of our life be for
him alone. We have only one task during the night
of the present life — to love Jesus.

I know that Jesus is in me — he it is who does
everything in me: I do nothing.

The nothingness of me is strangely loved;
Sustained ever
the all of love, my need, is strangely here;
Departing never.
We must love our nothingness, and think only of
the All which is infinitely loveable.

(*Daily Readings With Saint Therese of Lisieux*)

After reflecting on the prayer, contemplate the love relationship
that you have with Jesus. Share with Jesus your feelings of being
loved in your nothingness. What can you do to love your nothingness and grow in healthy self-esteem at the same time?

Day 2

Saint Francis of Assisi

Saint Francis of Assisi lived in the late twelfth and early thirteenth centuries. He is one of the most popular saints of all time. People have long admired his simplicity of life, love of people, and appreciation for all God's creatures.

As a young man Francis started out as something of a daredevil pleasure-seeker. The son of a wealthy silk merchant, Francis eagerly gallivanted off to war in hopes of being a big hero. However, when he was 20 the enemy threw him in prison. Soon after his release he became ill. During the illness he pledged to join the pope's armies. Later, on his journey to the papal armies, he encountered a man dressed in rags. Francis felt such compassion for him that he exchanged his expensive clothes for the rags. After this experience Francis decided not to join the pope's army but to return to Assisi and commit himself totally to living in accordance with the gospel.

Francis was indeed a charismatic personality. This gentle man's kindness appeals to many in our contemporary age who struggle to find peace amid violence and to preserve natural beauty amid pollution and toxic waste.

In his own time, though, Francis was seen as an eccentric. He stripped himself naked to show independence from his family and threw himself in thorn bushes to rid himself of temptations. His view of poverty was absolute. When some in his order advocated land ownership, Francis fought to keep them from acquiring property. He said:

My brothers, the Lord has called me to the way of simplicity and humbleness, and this is the way he has pointed out to me for myself and for those who will believe and follow me. The Lord told me that he would have me poor and foolish in this world, and he willed not to lead us by any other way than that. May God confound you by your own wisdom and learning and, for all your faultfinding, send you back to your vocation whether you will or not.

Prayer Suggestion: Read and pray the following reflection in the spirit of Saint Francis.

Peace Prayer of Saint Francis

Lord, make me an instrument of your peace,
where there is hatred, let me sow love,
where there is injury, pardon,
where there is doubt, faith,
where there is despair, hope,
where there is darkness, light,
and where there is sadness, joy.

O, Divine Master, grant that I may not so much seek
to be consoled as to console,
to be understood as to understand,
to be loved as to love.

For it is in giving that we receive;
it is in pardoning that we are pardoned;
and it is in dying that we are born to eternal life.

(Daily Readings With Saint Francis of Assisi)

Reflect on how Jesus is calling you to be an "instrument of peace" in your daily life. Share with Jesus your feelings and thoughts about this challenge. Decide on one practical way you will try to live out this prayer in your life.

Day 3

Saint Teresa of Avila

Saint Teresa of Avila was a Spaniard born in 1515. She grew up in the period of Spain's exploration of the New World to the west.

Teresa convinced her brother to accompany her to the land of the Moors to be martyred for the love of God. She wrote in her autobiography, "…and our Lord, I believe, had given us courage enough, even at so tender an age, if we could have found the means to proceed; but our greatest difficulty seemed to be our father and mother."

As an adolescent Teresa underwent some of the turmoil and temptations common to young people at this age. An attractive and popular young woman, Teresa enjoyed partying. After her mother died though, a stepsister supervised Teresa's social life. During this period Teresa was exposed to some negative influences which she later regretted, as her autobiography shows. In spite of her father's opposition, Teresa entered the Convent of the Incarnation at Avila in 1536. During her early years in religious life, Teresa struggled with her desires for frivolity and entertainment versus a deeper relationship with God. This continued until one day a picture of Christ in his Passion deeply moved Teresa. During the experience she concluded that she was blocking God's grace and love. She then decided to live a life of deep prayer and to found a house in which the Primitive Rule of the Order of Carmel would be observed. Undaunted by the opposition of some in her order, as well as many of the local people, Teresa opened her first convent in 1562. Before her death at the age of 67, Teresa had founded 15 more houses for the Discalced Carmelite nuns and two houses for friars in association with Saint John of the Cross. *Discalced* means "unshod" and is used to distinguish the stricter discipline of her reformed order from the earlier Calced congregations.

Two statements sum up Saint Teresa's approach to prayer: "Our Lord does not care so much for the importance of our works as for the love with which they are done" and "When we do all we can, His Majesty will enable us to do more every day." (From *The Interior Castle* by Saint Teresa of Avila.)

In recognition of her greatness as a spiritual mentor for people of all ages, the Church gave Teresa the title of "Doctor of the Church."

Prayer Suggestion: Reflect on the following prayer. After the prayer there are questions to help you in your reflection.

See Yourself in Him

If you feel happy, think of Our Lord at His Resurrection
for the very thought of how He rose from the tomb will delight you.
How He shone with splendour!
What spoils He brought away from the battle,
where He won a glorious kingdom that He wishes to make all your own
and Himself with it.
Is it much to look but once on Him Who gives you such riches?

If you have trials to bear, if you are sorrowful
watch Him on His way to the garden.
What grief must have arisen in His soul to cause Him,
who was patience itself to manifest and complain of it!

Or see Him bound to the column, full of sufferings,
His flesh all torn to pieces because of His tender love for
you.

Or look on Him laden with the cross,
and not allowed to stay to take a breath.

He will gaze on you with beautiful, compassionate eyes,
and will forget His own grief to solace yours,
only because you went to comfort Him,
and turned to look at Him.

(Daily Readings With Saint Teresa of Avila)

As you look at Jesus at his Resurrection, who is Jesus for *you*?
Savior? Your beloved? Friend? Deliverer? Refuge? Is he your
strength? Your brother? King? Comforter? As the risen Jesus looks
at you, how does he feel about you?

As you look at Jesus in his sufferings at Gethsemane, scourged
at the pillar, and on the Cross, who is Jesus for you?

Day 4

Saint John of the Cross

Saint John of the Cross was born in Castile, Spain, in 1542. His father came from a wealthy background but, because of his marriage to a working-class woman, he was disinherited. As a result John's father adopted his wife's trade of weaving in order to make a living. John had two brothers. One brother died in infancy, and the other was mentally retarded. In return for assisting a businessman in hospital work, John received an education in a Jesuit school.

At the age of 20, John entered the Carmelite Priory at Medina and studied for the priesthood at the University of Salamanca, one of the Spanish theological centers. After ordination in 1567, he met Teresa of Avila who at this time had just founded a convent of reformed Carmelite nuns in Avila and was attempting to persuade the men to do the same. When she met John in the fall of 1567, she was 52 and John was 25. Before they met John had been thinking about joining the Carthusians in pursuit of a more solitary life of prayer.

With Antonio, an elderly, like-minded friar, John initiated reform within his Calced Carmelite Order. However, some of those Calced Carmelites who were opposed to the reform kidnapped John and he ended up in prison in the Priory of Toledo. There, members of his own order publicly flogged, humiliated, and tortured John. It was during this time that he wrote a beautiful mystical poem inspired by the Song of Songs — *The Spiritual Canticle* — which describes the soul's union with God.

John eventually escaped from prison and then hid in the convent of the Carmelite nuns of Toledo until the controversy over the reform of Carmel quieted down.

Saints John of the Cross and Teresa of Avila remained close friends until her death. The Church regards both of them as Doctors of the Church and great spiritual teachers of mystical and contemplative prayer. Teresa and John exemplify the powerful partnership and deep love that women and men are called to share with one another in the spiritual journey.

In Saint John's writings he compares our union with God to the love between lover and beloved. In *The Living Flame of Love,* he uses the imagery of the Holy Spirit as a flame, burning and wounding as it gets the soul ready to be consumed in love's ecstatic fire. In *Dark Night of the Soul* John depicts faith as the guide that helps us trust God when we do not see, feel, or taste.

Prayer Suggestion: Relax your mind and body. Soft instrumental music may provide an excellent background for this prayer experience. If you'd like, try a centering exercise such as focusing on your breathing or repeating a prayer word or phrase such as "Jesus, Abba, my beloved, my delight, living flame of love."

Read slowly the translation of *The Living Flame of Love* below. Pause at any metaphors or poetic images that touch you.

The Living Flame of Love

O living flame of love
that tenderly woundest my soul in its deepest centre,
Since thou art no longer oppressive,
perfect me now if it be thy will,
Break the web of this sweet encounter.

Oh sweet burn!
Oh, delectable wound!
Oh, soft hand!
Oh, delicate touch
That savours of eternal life and pays every debt!
In slaying, thou hast changed death into life.

Oh, lamps of fire,
in whose splendours the deep caverns of sense which were
dark and blind

With strange brightness
Give heat and light together to their Beloved!

How gently and lovingly thou awakenest in my bosom,
Where thou dwellest secretly and alone!
And in thy sweet breathing, full of blessing and glory,
How delicately thou inspirest my love!

Imagine, see, and feel God the living
flame "delicately touching" you, "tenderly wounding" you. How do you
feel? What is your response?

Is there a situation in your life or a
part of you that needs God's "delicate
touch"? What do you feel as God's
"soft hand" touches and holds you?

Day 5

Blessed Julian of Norwich

Julian of Norwich was born in 1342 in England. She was probably educated by the nuns at Carrow, a Benedictine priory, although she refers to herself as "unlettered."

During a serious illness in 1373 Julian received the 16 "shewings" or revelations of the Lord. She became an "anchoress" — a woman consecrated to God, living permanently alone in a small room attached to Saint Julian's Church in Norwich. Julian probably took her name from the church that, in those days, would have been 400 years old. For the next 20 years Julian reflected on the vision and its meaning in her book *Revelations of Divine Love*. This was the first English language book written by a woman and is a spiritual classic. (See the two-volume book *Daily Readings With Julian of Norwich* .)

In *Revelations of Divine Love*, Julian uses many beautiful images to describe God's love. Her famous images of the motherhood of God and Jesus describe the totality of this love in a fresh and appealing way. In her writing, Jesus is the Christ-mother because he is the one who bears his children into everlasting life. Julian's writing is filled with feminine images of the Trinity, something that today's woman can find quite relevant.

Julian wrote in *Revelations of Divine Love*:

When our Lord in his courtesy and grace shows himself to the soul, we have what we desire. Then we care no longer about praying for any thing, for our whole strength and aim is set on beholding. This is prayer, high and ineffable, in my eyes.

Julian viewed prayer as a journey into the love of God and all creation. For her, even the hazelnut was a reminder of God's sustaining presence in all things. She firmly believed that nothing, not even sin or the painful sufferings of this life, need separate us from God's love.

Prayer Suggestion: Reflect on the following prayer of Julian's.

God, Our Father and Mother

As truly as God is our father, so just as truly is he our mother.

In our father, God Almighty, we have our being;
In our merciful mother we are remade and restored.
Our fragmented lives are knit together and made perfect....
And by giving and yielding ourselves, through grace, to the
Holy Spirit we are made whole.

It is I, the strength and goodness of fatherhood.
It is I, the wisdom of motherhood.
It is I, the light and grace of holy love.
It is I, the Trinity, it is I, the unity.
I am the sovereign goodness in all things.
It is I who teach you to love.
It is I who teach you to desire.
It is I who am the reward of all true desiring.
(Daily Readings With Julian of Norwich, Vol. 1)

Now, reflect on the meaning of God as father. What images, thoughts, and feelings arise as you meditate on this reality? Share with God your reactions and be attentive to God's response.

Reflect on the meaning of God as mother. What images, thoughts, and feelings arise as you reflect on this reality? Share with God your reactions and be attentive to God's response.

Do you experience God's love as both fatherly and motherly? If so, thank God for that total divine love.

Day 6

Saint Bonaventure

In 1221 Saint Bonaventure was born in Bagnorea, a small town in Italy. While Bonaventure was a child, Saint Francis of Assisi died in 1226.

Even though it is unlikely that Bonaventure ever met Francis, Bonaventure did write about a healing he received:

> When I was a boy, as I still vividly remember, I was snatched from the jaws of death by [Francis'] invocation and merits. So if I remained silent and did not sing his praises, I fear that I would be rightly accused of the crime of ingratitude. I recognize that God saved my life through his power in my very person.

*(Bonaventure: The Soul's Journey Into God:
the Tree of Life, the Life of Francis)*

At the age of 17 Bonaventure began studies at the University of Paris. The Franciscans greatly influenced him there, and he eventually entered the Franciscan Order and studied theology under the renowned Franciscan scholar Alexander of Hales. Although Bonaventure remained an intellectual, the simplicity of Saint Francis of Assisi captivated him.

In 1254 Bonaventure became a master in theology and assumed leadership of the Franciscan school in Paris. He taught there until elected minister general of the Franciscans' Friars Minor in 1257. Through his personal holiness and gifts of reconciliation, Bonaventure brought unity and healing to different factions within his community, thus earning the title of "Second Founder of the Franciscans."

In 1273 Pope Gregory X appointed Bonaventure cardinal-bishop of Albano. Bonaventure then helped prepare for the Council of Lyons. Bonaventure played a role in implementing this council's reforms and promoted the reconciliation of the secular clergy with the mendicant orders. Bonaventure died at the council on July 15, 1274. In 1482 Pope Sixtus IV canonized Bonaventure and declared him to be a Doctor of the Universal Church with the title "Doctor Seraphicus" — Angelic Doctor.

Prayer Suggestion: Imaginatively enter into the following exerpt's verses, imagery, and truth. Pay particular attention to the concepts of "Christ...the way and the door," "the Mercy Seat placed above the ark of God," and "hidden manna."

From *The Soul's Journey Into God*

Christ is the way and the door;
Christ is the ladder and the vehicle,
Like the mercy Seat placed above the ark of God
and the mystery hidden from eternity.

Whoever turns his face fully to the Mercy Seat
and with faith, hope and love,
devotion, admiration, exultation,
appreciation, praise, and joy
beholds him hanging upon the cross,
such a one makes the Pasch, that is, the passover,
with Christ.
By the staff of the cross
he passes over the Red Sea,
going from Egypt into the desert,
where he will taste the hidden manna;
and with Christ
he rests in the tomb,
as if dead to the outer world,
but experiencing,
as far as is possible in this wayfarer's state,
what was said on the cross
to the thief who adhered to Christ;
Today you shall be with me in paradise.

Share with God your thoughts and feelings about the passage on the previous page. How is Christ "the way and the door" in your life? What difficult areas in our contemporary world need Christ to be "the way and door"?

How have you experienced God's love "like the Mercy Seat placed above the ark of God" and the "mystery hidden from eternity"?

How would you feel if Christ said to you: "Today you shall be with me in paradise"? Loved? Anxious? Joyful? Fearful?

Day 7

Saint Catherine of Siena

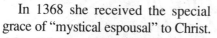

Catherine was born in 1347 in Siena, Italy, the second youngest of 25 children. According to legend, Catherine was a pleasant, vivacious, idealistic, stubborn, and independent child. At the age of seven she vowed her virginity to God, and at fifteen she cut her hair off in rebellion against family efforts to force her to marry. At age 16 she became a Dominican tertiary.

In 1368 she received the special grace of "mystical espousal" to Christ. After this experience she left the solitude of her bedroom and returned to the normal activities of her family. She then began a life of service to the sick and poor of Siena.

During this time Catherine attracted many followers and friends who formed a spiritual community that gathered in her room to discuss theology, Scripture, and spiritual life. In 1374 Catherine met Raymond of Capua, who became her spiritual director and lifelong friend.

Catherine's prayer life had a definite impact on Raymond. He eventually wrote her biography *Legenda Major* — "Major Legend." In it he wrote,

Being so closely associated with her I was able to see at firsthand how, as soon as she was freed from the occupations in which she was engaged for the work of souls, at once one might also say a natural process, her mind was raised to the things of heaven.

Catherine and Raymond describe the friendship they share as resulting from a special faith they have in each other that is deeply rooted in their faith in God. Catherine says to Raymond:

Just as love for neighbor proceeds from love for God, so does faith concerning creatures proceed from this love, whether it be general faith or special faith....That special faith results in so much love that it cannot believe or imagine that either one of us could wish anything else than the other's good.

(Catherine of Siena as Seen in Her Letters)

Catherine and Raymond worked together helping victims of the plague which struck Siena in the summer of 1374. Caring for the sick and dying, Catherine and Raymond provide us with a beautiful example of women and men as partners in ministry.

Catherine lived in an age of social and political tension between the Italian city-states and the papacy. She worked courageously as a negotiator to restore peace in the Church. In 1376 Catherine traveled to Avignon to plead the cause of reconciliation between the city-state of Florence and Pope Gregory XI, only to be betrayed by the Florentines who disowned her and sent another emissary to represent them. In spite of this disappointment Catherine continued to work for peace and unity in the Church. Other causes that attracted Catherine's attentions were clergy reform and returning the papacy to Rome.

Catherine advocated loyalty and unity in an age of tension and dissent within the Church's history. Popes and cardinals trusted her advice. Always a loyal daughter of the Church, Catherine nevertheless advocated reform in the Church. As a result, centuries later Pope Paul VI honored her with the title "Doctor of the Church" in 1970.

Many people today refer to Catherine as the "social mystic," or a "mystic activist" because of her refusal to compromise truth as she experienced it. Her ministry grew out of her contemplation.

Catherine is a model of a holy woman who successfully integrated social action and contemplation. She also worked with the poor to improve the quality of their lives and prayer.

Prayer Suggestion: Below is an excerpt from Catherine's greatest work, *The Dialogue*. Though it is profitable to meditate on the following passage that is from Catherine's teaching on the mystical life, you may find it more helpful to read and prayerfully reflect on the entirety of her work in *Catherine of Siena: The Dialogue*. It is part of the *Classics of Western Spirituality Series* published by Paulist Press.

Pray this selection from *The Dialogue* for as many days as you feel drawn to do so. Spend time on each phrase, verse, or image in which you were feeling the greatest attraction. Select one phrase, image, or verse that touches you and express your love, gratitude, or joy to God in any of the following ways: words, song, poetry, music, dance, or in some other art form such as drawing, painting, sculpting, and so forth.

The Dialogue

Then that soul was as if drunk with love of true holy poverty. She was filled to bursting in the supreme eternal magnificence and so transformed in the abyss of his supreme and immeasurable providence that though she was in the vessel of her body it seemed as if the fire of charity within her had taken over and rapt her outside her body. And with her mind's eye steadily fixed on the divine majesty she spoke to the eternal Father:

O eternal Father! O fiery abyss of charity! O eternal beauty, O eternal wisdom, O eternal goodness, O eternal mercy! O hope and refuge of sinners! O immeasurable generosity! O eternal infinite Good! O mad lover! And you have need of your creature? It seems to me, for you act as if you could not live without her, in spite of the facts that are Life itself, and everything has life from you and can have life without you. When then are you so mad? Because you have fallen in love with what you have made! You are pleased and delighted over her within yourself, as if you were drunk [with desire] for her salvation. She runs away from you and you go looking for her. She strays and you draw closer to her. You clothed yourself in our humanity, and nearer than you could not have come. (From *Catherine of Siena: The Dialogue*.)

The Dialogue portrays poetic images and descriptions of God's love like, "O fiery abyss of charity," "O hope and refuge of sinners!" and "O mad lover!"

Let God share with you how these qualities of divine love have been demonstrated throughout your life. Compose your own litany of praise as Catherine did in *The Dialogue*. Obtain a copy of *The Dialogue*, and continue to share in the richness of Catherine's mystical prayer.

CHAPTER SEVEN

◆

PRAYING
With Mary

$\boxed{T}$he rosary has been a favorite devotion in Catholic life for centuries. According to popular legend Saint Dominic received the rosary from the Blessed Mother. However, most historians believe that the rosary developed gradually during the time from the 1100s to 1569, when Pope Pius V officially recommended this prayer of "150 angelic salutations…with the Lord's Prayer at each decade… while meditating on the mysteries which recall the entire life of our Lord Jesus Christ." This pope added the second part to the Hail Mary, and this form of the prayer was adopted for the rosary.

The rosary developed out of the laity's need for a prayer form similar to the Psalter — the 150 psalms that monks prayed. During the Middle Ages some people who were unable to read developed the practice of reciting 150 Our Fathers. Others recited Our Lady's Psalter, which consisted of 150 Ave Marias (the angel Gabriel's greeting to Mary), interspersed with verses from the psalms. Over time, the focus of the rosary became meditation on the mysteries from the life of Christ. The rosary took its present form between the fourteenth and fifteenth centuries when a Carthusian monk divided the 150 Ave Marias into the 15 decades, with each decade preceded by the Our Father. During the next 400 years the rosary consisting of 15 decades (or 150 Hail Marys) remained basically the same. In our contemporary era, however, people usually pray the five-decade rosary rather than all fifteen decades.

During her earthly life, Mary pondered God's ways, reflecting on them in her heart. "He went down with them and came to Nazareth, and was obedient to them; and his mother kept all these things in her heart" (Luke 2:51). With Mary we can relive the 15 mysteries of Jesus' life from his Conception and Birth until his Death and Resurrection. Jesus gave Mary to us during his final dying moments on the Cross: "When Jesus saw his mother and the disciple there whom he loved, he said to his mother, 'Woman, behold, your son.' Then he said to the disciple, 'Behold, your mother.' And from that hour the disciple took her into his home" (John 19:26-27).

Mary is both mother and companion to each of us. With great tenderness and love she walks with us on our spiritual journey to God's heart. By praying the rosary in the company of Mary we gain a deeper appreciation for Christ's saving work in the mystery of redemption. The rosary's 15 mysteries focus on the joy, sorrow, and glory of Jesus' life.

In this chapter you will focus mainly on praying the Joyful Mysteries. As you pray, surrender your tensions, worries, and anxieties to God and allow the rhythmic, repetitive recitation of the Our Father and the Hail Mary to focus your heart on the joy-filled mysteries of Christ's life. They can give new meaning to your life, too.

HOW TO USE THIS PRAYER FORM

To pray the Joyful Mysteries, begin with the first three beads on the rosary and recite on these beads the Apostles' Creed, one Our Father, three Hail Marys, and one Glory Be to the Father. Then, moving your hand along the beads, recite one Our Father, ten Hail Marys, and one Glory Be to the Father as you meditate on each of the five Joyful Mysteries of Jesus' life. The repetition and rhythm of "Hail Mary...Holy Mary..." can relax the mind and center your heart on God's work in the central mysteries of Christ's life, death, and glory.

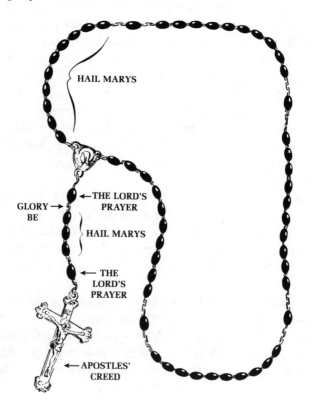

HAIL MARYS

GLORY → BE

←THE LORD'S PRAYER

HAIL MARYS

← THE LORD'S PRAYER

← APOSTLES' CREED

At left is one possible approach to praying with Mary the Joyful Mysteries of Jesus' life and the joyful mysteries of your life. For the last two days of the week you'll find two popular prayers, the Memorare and the Magnificat.

The Memorare is a prayer to Mary which Saint Bernard wrote. Catholics have prayed it since the twelfth century. The Magnificat is Mary's canticle of praise found in the Gospel of Luke.

All of us can develop a deeper love for Jesus by praying with Mary. As you meditate with her on the Joyful Mysteries in Jesus' life, you can gain new insights into your own journey in faith. The five Joyful Mysteries present a blueprint for happiness and show where you can look to find joy in everyday life. With Mary as your Mother and companion to guide you, you will discover rich treasures that will help you become a Christ-bearer and witness of the gospel in today's world.

The prayer plan for the next seven days will involve meditating on the five Joyful Mysteries and two other Marian prayers. One or more prayer suggestions are listed under each day. Since there are several choices for each Joyful Mystery of the rosary listed under Days 1 through 5, you might desire to pray the rosary in one sitting, choosing the selections that most appeal to you. Or you might decide to spend more time on one mystery and combine several suggestions to help you delve more deeply into that particular mystery. Some people might benefit from experimenting with different suggestions for each mystery each time they pray the Joyful Mysteries, the Memorare, or the Magnificat. There are many possibilities for creativity here. Choose those suggestions that enhance your prayer life and draw you closer to God.

The Joyful Mysteries are the Annunciation, the Visitation, the Birth of Jesus, the Presentation, and the Finding in the Temple. For more information on the Glorious and Sorrowful Mysteries, as well as the rosary in general, see the pamphlet *Let's Pray (Not Just Say) the Rosary* published by Liguori Publications.

Day 1

The Annunciation

Reflect on the first Joyful Mystery, the Annunciation. Read the following story of the angel Gabriel's visit to Mary in which he announced the good news:

> In the sixth month, the angel Gabriel was sent from God to a town of Galilee called Nazareth, to a virgin betrothed to a man named Joseph, of the house of David, and the virgin's name was Mary. And coming to her, he said, "Hail, favored one! The Lord is with you." But she was greatly troubled at what was said and pondered what sort of greeting this might be. Then the angel said to her, "Do not be afraid, Mary, for you have found favor with God. Behold, you will conceive in your womb and bear a son, and you shall name him Jesus. He will be great and will be called Son of the Most High, and the Lord God will give him the throne of David his father, and he will rule over the house of Jacob forever, and of his kingdom there will be no end." But Mary said to the angel, "How can this be, since I have no relations with a man?"
>
> (Luke 1:26-34)

Prayer Suggestions: Reflect on Mary's feelings as she heard this announcement. How would you have felt if you were Mary? Would you have said "yes" to God?

In spite of your fears and anxieties about the future, can you say with Mary at this moment in your life, "I am the handmaid of the Lord. May it be done to me according to your word?" (Luke 1:38). Share your thoughts and feelings with Mary.

Select one joyful memory in which you felt God selected you for some special relationship, mission, or work. It could be your wedding day, the day you completed a significant project at work, selection of a special ministry, and so forth. How did you feel when you said "yes" to God? Fearful? Joyful? Peaceful? Sad? Hopeful? Can you, like Mary, accept your goodness and giftedness? You are made in God's image. All that you are is God's gift to you. All that you become is your gift to God.

As you recite one Our Father, ten Hail Marys, and one Glory Be to the Father, share your thoughts and feelings with Mary.

Listen to Mary's response to your joyful memory. Allow Mary to share her thoughts and feelings with you. Spend some time praying with Mary — praising and thanking Jesus for this joyful memory.

Day 2

The Visitation

Read and meditate on the story of Mary's visit to Elizabeth found in Luke 1:39-45. Some of it appears below.

> When Elizabeth heard Mary's greeting, the infant leaped in her womb, and Elizabeth, filled with the holy Spirit, cried out in a loud voice and said, "Most blessed are you among women, and blessed is the fruit of your womb. And how does this happen to me, that the mother of my Lord should come to me?"
>
> (Luke 1:41-43)

Prayer Suggestions: Reflect on Mary's feelings as she shared her God and her joy with her cousin Elizabeth. How would you have felt if you were Mary? How would you have felt if you were Elizabeth? How can you share unselfish love with others? How can you bring others joy by giving them your time, energy, and love? Share your thoughts and feelings with Mary and Elizabeth.

Listen to Mary's and Elizabeth's responses to you. Allow them to share their thoughts and feelings with you.

Reflect on a recent encounter in which you have been a channel of God's joy. Share this special moment, event, or relationship with Mary and/or ask Mary to help you become aware of any person who may need you to bring Jesus to them at this time.

What does Mary's act of kindness teach us about reaching out in love to the poor or needy? Decide on one act of loving service you can do to lighten someone else's burden.

Spend some time praying with Mary — praising and thanking Jesus for this joyful encounter and/or new possibility of loving service.

Day 3

The Birth of Jesus

Read and meditate on the story of Jesus' birth found in Luke 2:1-20; Matthew 1:18—2:12. Some of it appears below.

While they were there, the time came for her to have her child, and she gave birth to her firstborn son. She wrapped him in swaddling clothes and laid him in a manger, because there was no room for them in the inn.

(Luke 2:6-7)

Prayer Suggestions: Reflect on Mary's feelings as she gave birth to Jesus. How would you have felt if you were Mary? How would you have felt if you were Joseph? If you could have been there what would you have said to Mary? To Joseph? To Jesus? Share your thoughts and feelings with Jesus, Mary, and Joseph.

Reflect on a time in your life when you were a Christ-bearer — one who brought God's love, forgiveness, and healing to another or others. When did the Word become flesh through you? How did you feel? Fearful? Joyful? Anxious? Happy? Peaceful?

Reflect on a time in your life when someone else was a Christ-bearer to you. How did you feel? Fearful? Joyful? Anxious? Happy? Peaceful?

Pray with Mary that you may become more sensitive to opportunities in your life to be a Christ-bearer to another/others.

Day 4

The Presentation of Jesus in the Temple

Read and meditate on the Presentation of Jesus in the Temple in Luke 2:22-35. Some of it is found below.

When the days were completed for their purification according to the law of Moses, they took him up to Jerusalem to present him to the Lord, just as it is written in the law of the Lord, "Every male that opens the womb shall be consecrated to the Lord," and to offer the sacrifice of "a pair of turtledoves or two young pigeons," in accordance with the dictate in the law of the Lord.

(Luke 2:22-24)

Prayer Suggestions: Reflect on Mary's and Joseph's feelings as they consecrated Jesus to God in the temple. How did you think Mary felt as she listened to Simeon's prophecy: "Behold, this child is destined for the fall and rise of many in Israel, and to be a sign that will be contradicted (and you yourself a sword will pierce) so that the thoughts of many hearts may be revealed" (Luke 2:34-35).

Share your thoughts and feelings about this prophecy with Mary and Joseph.

Reflect on a time in your life when you had an opportunity to do something special for God — to give back to God the gift that God had first given to you. Were you able to present this gift to God with open hands and a grateful heart? To present to the Lord means to bless — to give back to God what God has first given you. Can you consecrate all that you are, all your possessions, all your relationships, to God?

Spend some time praying with Mary. Praise and thank Jesus for all that you are, all your possessions, all your relationships. Consecrate and bless each one, giving back to God what God first gave to you.

Reflect on the *Dedication of a Family to Mary* found on the next page. When you pray, surrender your entire being to God.

Dedication of a Family to Mary

Blessed and immaculate Virgin, our queen and mother, you are the refuge and consolation of all those who are in need. I bow in humility before you and with my family choose you for my lady, mother, and advocate with God.

I dedicate myself, and all who belong to me, forever to your service and beg you, dear mother of God, to receive us into the number of your servants.

Take us all under your protection. Graciously aid us now in life and still more at the hour of death.

Mother of Mercy, I choose you lady and queen of my whole house, my relatives, my interests, and all my affairs.

Take care of them; intercede for them all as it pleases you. Bless me and all my family, and do not permit any of us to offend your Son.

Defend us in temptations;
Deliver us from doubts;
Console us in afflictions;

Be with us in sickness, and especially in the hour of death. Grant that we may come to you in heaven to thank you, and together with you praise and love our redeemer, Jesus, for all eternity.

(Saint Alphonsus Liguori in *Mother's Manual*
by A. Francis Coomes, S.J.)

Day 5

The Finding of Jesus in the Temple

Read and meditate on the Finding of Jesus in the Temple in the passage below.

Each year his parents went to Jerusalem for the feast of Passover, and when he was twelve years old, they went up according to festival custom. After they had completed its days, as they were returning, the boy Jesus remained behind in Jerusalem, but his parents did not know it. Thinking that he was in the caravan, they journeyed for a day and looked for him among their relatives and acquaintances, but not finding him, they returned to Jerusalem to look for him. After three days they found him in the temple, sitting in the midst of the teachers, listening to them and asking them questions, and all who heard him were astounded at his understanding and his answers. When his parents saw him, they were astonished, and his mother said to him, "Son, why have you

done this to us? Your father and I have been looking for you with great anxiety." And he said to them, "Why were you looking for me? Did you not know that I must be in my Father's house?" But they did not understand what he said to them. He went down with them and came to Nazareth, and was obedient to them; and his mother kept all these things in her heart.

(Luke 2:41-51)

Prayer Suggestion: Could you, like Jesus, Mary, and Joseph, experience joy in pain? Could you believe and yet not understand? Could you risk the misunderstanding and hurt of loved ones in order to do God's will? Would you be able to trust during times of darkness, suffering, and mourning? How can reflecting on this Joyful Mystery give you courage in the midst of resignation, confusion, anger, and pain?

Spend some time praying with Mary. Praise and thank Jesus for the opportunities you have had and will have to believe and act like Mary and Joseph during times of darkness and suffering. Ask for the ability to do God's will, even if it means family and friends will misunderstand or feel hurt. Ask Mary to pray with you that you may live your faith even when *you* do not understand. Ask that you may trust God's love for you, no matter how dark the situation may appear.

We lose our joy when we turn away from Christ by deliberate sin. Mary understands that we do not always make wise choices. She loves us even when we lose our way. Ask her to be with you in moments of sin and failure to remind you of God's boundless mercy. Be open to the amazing grace of Jesus, our Savior, who always forgives and heals the deepest wounds of our hearts.

Day 6

The Memorare

Remember, O most gracious Virgin Mary,
that never was it known
that anyone who fled to your protection,
implored your help,
or sought your intercession,
was left unaided.

Inspired with this confidence, I fly to you,
O Virgin of virgins, my Mother.
To you I come, before you I stand,
sinful and sorrowful.

O Mother of the Word Incarnate,
despise not my petitions,
but in your mercy hear and answer me.
Amen.

Prayer Suggestion: Make an intercessory prayer list of people and situations that concern you. Share with Mary your thoughts and feelings about each person and situation on the list. Talk with her, addressing her as a loving Mother who cares deeply for you.

Ask her to pray to Jesus with you for each person and intention on your list. As a sign of your love and trust in Mary, your loving Mother, pray the Memorare often.

Day 7

The Magnificat

The Magnificat is comprised of the following verses found in Scripture.

My soul proclaims the greatness of the Lord;
  my spirit rejoices in God my savior.
For he has looked upon his handmaid's lowliness;
  behold, from now on will all ages call me blessed.
The Mighty One has done great things for me,
  and holy is his name.
His mercy is from age to age
  to those who fear him.
He has shown might with his arm,
  dispersed the arrogant of mind and heart.
He has thrown down the rulers from their thrones
  but lifted up the lowly.
The hungry he has filled with good things;
  the rich he has sent away empty.
He has helped Israel his servant,
  remembering his mercy,
according to his promise to our fathers,
  to Abraham and to his descendants forever.

(Luke 1:46-55)

Prayer Suggestions: Select one line of the Magnificat. Throughout the day pray this line with Mary as a mantra to remind you of God's loving presence. During this prayer week you could select a different line of the Magnificat for each day.

As you pray the Magnificat, try to understand the thoughts and feelings of Mary as she prayed this canticle of praise. Create a dialogue with Mary in your prayer journal.

Write your own Magnificat — your prayer of praise for all the wondrous things God has done for you. Share it with Mary.

Reflect on the Magnificat as a prayer of liberation for the poor, for the oppressed, for minorities, for women. How does Mary's canticle provide us with a model of Christian prayer for the contemporary Church?

CHAPTER EIGHT

◆

PRAYING
With the Church

As Christians we believe in a personal God who is active in everyday experience. We believe that God creates, activates, and loves. God does not just "love" all people in a general sense but also loves each of us individually as if there were only one of us. In the Scriptures we encounter a God who is deeply in love with us. In the Old Testament we meet a God who calls us by name, who hurts when we turn away, who forgives us tenderly, and who loves us unconditionally. The New Testament reveals a God who shows the immensity of divine love by becoming a human being in the person of Jesus.

Jesus grew up in a family, experienced human feelings, made decisions, and was like us in all things but sin. Jesus shows the fullness of God's self-giving love by his suffering and dying on the Cross and rising from the dead. God continues to love us passionately and is with us now in the Holy Spirit. The Holy Spirit is the presence and power of God — the very breath of God's life in each of us. The Spirit is at work liberating, healing, transforming, and empowering each of us so that we may bear witness to the Good News of the gospel in our lives. As Christians we do not journey alone. We are joined together as a Christian community that expresses our beliefs in the one God who is Father, Son, and Spirit. We share a way of life — a way of loving with the risen Jesus in the power of the Spirit. As one Body — the Church — we join together in faith to share Word, worship, and construction of the kingdom. We are sustained on this journey by our faith. Our faith is the communal statement of belief — the Creed.

The Nicene Creed *is* the Church's statement of faith. It is rooted in the proclamation of faith that new Christians expressed at their Baptism.

The First Council of Nicea formulated the Nicene Creed in the year 325. The Creed summarizes the beliefs proclaimed by Christians from the earliest days of the Church. Its four principal statements of belief in the Father, the Son, the Spirit, and the Church provide an outline of the essential doctrines of the Catholic faith.

In this chapter you will have the opportunity to explore a variety of ways of praying the Creed as both a personal and communal statement of faith. As you do this you will experience the breadth, length, and height of God's love.

HOW TO USE THIS METHOD

The prayer suggestions mentioned for each day invite you to utilize your intellect, senses, imagination, mind, heart, and feelings. They are designed to help you grow in a greater understanding of the divine truths of God's love expressed in the Church's communal statement of faith. They're also designed to engage your imagination and heart in an intimate experience of God's love.

The Nicene Creed

We believe in one God,
  the Father, the Almighty,
  maker of heaven and earth,
  of all that is seen and unseen.

We believe in one Lord, Jesus Christ,
  the only Son of God,
  eternally begotten of the Father,
  God from God, Light from Light,
  true God from true God,
  begotten, not made, one in Being with the Father.
  Through him all things were made.
  For us and for our salvation he came down from heaven:
by the power of the Holy Spirit
  he was born of the Virgin Mary, and became man.

For our sake he was crucified under Pontius Pilate;
   he suffered, died, and was buried.
   On the third day he rose again
      in fulfillment of the Scriptures;
   he ascended into heaven
      and is seated at the right hand of the Father.
He will come again in glory to judge the living
      and the dead,
   and his kingdom will have no end.

We believe in the Holy Spirit, the Lord, the giver of life,
   who proceeds from the Father and the Son.
   With the Father and the Son he is worshiped
      and glorified.
   He has spoken through the Prophets.
   We believe in one holy catholic and apostolic Church.
   We acknowledge one baptism for the forgiveness of sins.
   We look for the resurrection of the dead,
      and the life of the world to come. Amen.

Day 1

We believe in one God,
  the Father, the Almighty,
  maker of heaven and earth,
  of all that is seen and unseen.

Prayer Suggestions: Find a quiet place where you want to walk. As you walk, open yourself to what is happening in the world. Notice the beauty in color, design, and texture of the sky, earth, trees, animals, flowers, plants, and so forth. Listen to the sounds and smell the aromas that strike you. Inhale the air that surrounds you and exhale deeply. Feel the sun, breeze, or wind and how it affects your body. Rest and enjoy the beauty of creation. There is no agenda — nothing that you must do but simply *be* in love with the God who has created everything around you.

Take a nature walk. Bring your camera and take pictures of God's gifts of creation. Make a collage with these pictures as a reminder of special scenes that evoked in you feelings of joy, peace, and beauty. You can utilize these pictures in future meditations on the beauty of God's creation.

Take a walk in a town or city. As you walk, praise God for the gifts of creation you see in the people around you and the things they have created. Many of us enjoy so-called "people watching" — an experience that easily lends itself to prayer. With it you can gain a real appreciation for the mundane but good people and things surrounding you every day that are easily taken for granted. Think of what we'd all be missing if we didn't have ordinary things like newspapers, garbage cans, grocery stores, bakeries, hospitals, schools, fire and police stations.

Thank God for the gift of ordinary people such as teachers, chefs, nurses, doctors, salesclerks, artists, garbage collectors, fire fighters, police officers, social workers, members of the armed forces, and so forth.

Day 2

I walk with beauty before me.
I walk with beauty behind me.
I walk with beauty below me.
I walk with beauty above me.
I walk with beauty all around me.

(Navajo Prayer)

Prayer Suggestions: Select one line from the Navajo Prayer as a centering prayer. Repeat it throughout the day to increase your awareness of God's presence.

Read one of the biblical accounts of creation in the first and second chapters of Genesis. Spend some time contemplating God's goodness and love present all around you. Write your own psalm or prayer of praise for the wonders of God's beautiful world.

Choose one or more of God's gifts of creation to contemplate. Look at the morning sunrise or evening sunset, a budding rose, a bird, a cloudy sky, green grass, and so forth. Allow the beauty of God's love to touch the depths of your being in one or more of God's gifts of creation. The following reflection expresses a profound experience of awe and wonder. Have you ever felt this way? Select a musical piece that reminds you of the grandeur of creation and play it as you reflect on the following prayer.

Heaven and Earth

It was as if lightning flashed into my spirit,
and I thought in my heart that the people around
me had seen it too, but they had not, and with
the light such a powerful peace and joy came into my heart.
In one moment I felt as if wholly revitalized by some
  infinite
power, so that my body would be shattered
    like an earthen vessel.
I saw God's Word weaving understanding,
the exceeding greatness of His power...
I could gladly seal with my blood the truth of those words:
Holy!
Wonderful!
Holy!
Wonderful!
Holy!
Eternally Wonderful!
I felt as if my body and soul were being lifted from the
    earth, and being dissolved to go to heaven...
Tears of joy flowed spontaneously from my eyes
    in torrents...
I felt a fullness within me.
If I slept it was but a little all night, I could only praise and
    wonder at God, and who could do less?
Because it had become heaven to me on earth; thank God
from my heart!...I cannot reckon it as one of the days of
earth, only as one of the days of heaven.

(Daily Readings from Prayers and Praises
in the Celtic Tradition, edited by A.M. Allchin
and Esther de Waal)

Day 3

We believe in one Lord, Jesus Christ,
the only Son of God,
eternally begotten of the Father,
God from God, Light from Light,
true God from true God,
begotten, not made, one in Being with the Father.
Through him all things were made.
For us and for our salvation
he came down from heaven:
by the power of the Holy Spirit
he was born of the Virgin Mary, and became man.

Prayer Suggestion: God revealed divine love to us in the person of Jesus Christ, the Word made flesh. Jesus shared all our human characteristics and feelings. In the gospels we find a description of the human experiences of Jesus.

Select from the list on the next page a story that describes a feeling or human characteristic of Jesus. Reflect on the meaning of this story. Use the questions listed on the next page to assist you. If you wish to meditate on each gospel story in depth, you might benefit from spreading your prayerful reflections over several weeks. You may wish to try recording your daily insights in a prayer journal. This has the advantage of providing a tool which can be used at another time for further prayer, reflection, and sharing with others.

Scripture Selections Showing

- Jesus as compassionate: Matthew 9:36
- Jesus as angry: Matthew 21:12-13, Mark 3:5
- Jesus as perturbed and troubled: John 11:33
- Jesus as tempted: Matthew 4:1-11
- Jesus crying: John 11:35-36
- Jesus as loving: Mark 10:21
- Jesus as emotionally overwrought: Mark 14:32-42; Luke 22:44

Questions

1. With which human feelings of Jesus do you identify?
2. Which human feelings of Jesus do you share?
3. Which qualities of Jesus attract you?
4. How can you grow to be more like Jesus?

Day 4

Miracle Stories

Read some or all of the miracle stories involving Jesus that are listed below.

- Cleansing of a leper: Matthew 8:1-4
- Healing of a centurion's servant: Matthew 8:5-13
- Healing of Jairus' daughter and the woman with a hemorrhage: Mark 5:21-43
- Healing of a deaf man: Mark 7:31-37
- Miraculous catch of fish: Luke 5:1-11
- Cleansing of a leper: Luke 5:12-15
- Healing of an infirm man at Bethesda: John 5:1-9
- Walking on the water: John 6:16-21

Prayer Suggestion: Select a miracle story from the list on page 104. Reflect on the meaning of the miracle. Use the questions below to assist you. If you wish to meditate on each miracle story in depth, you might benefit from spreading your prayerful reflections over several days. Some people might wish to record their insights for each day in a prayer journal. This has the advantage of providing a tool which can be used at another time for further prayer, reflection, and sharing with others.

1. How did the person feel before and after experiencing God's healing power in Jesus?

2. What would you have thought and/or felt if you had been the person who was healed?

3. Do you believe that Jesus continues to liberate, save, and heal people today?

4. Do you believe that Jesus wants to liberate, save, and heal you?

5. What areas of your life need the liberating, saving, healing touch of Jesus?

Day 5

We believe in the Holy Spirit, the Lord, the giver of life,
   who proceeds from the Father and the Son.
   With the Father and the Son he is worshiped and
      glorified.
   He has spoken through the Prophets.

Prayer Suggestions:
1. Pray and reflect on the following Scripture verses which describe the effects of the Holy Spirit.
- The creation of humanity: Genesis 2:7
- The story of Elijah: 1 Kings 19:9-13
- Dry bones: Ezekiel 37:1-14
- The story of Nicodemus: John 3:1-8
- The Holy Spirit's descent at Pentecost: Acts 2:1-4

2. Read and reflect on the promise God makes in the following Scripture passages.
- Ezekiel 36:26-27
- Jeremiah 31:31-34
- Joel 3:1-2
- John 14:10-20
- Luke 4:14-21

3. Read and reflect on the following Scripture selections. They refer to how Jesus and the Holy Spirit act to transform people's lives.
- Acts 3:1-16
- Acts 5:12-16
- Acts 9:1-19, 32-35, 36-42
- Acts 10:44-49
- Acts 8:14-25

Day 6

As Christians we believe the Spirit is always with us — guiding, prompting, and leading us. At our Confirmation the bishop laid hands on us and asked the Holy Spirit to empower us with gifts to serve the Christian community — the Body of Christ.

Prayer Suggestions:
1. Reflect on the meaning of this sacrament in your life. How has the Spirit used you to build the kingdom of God? In what areas of witness and service are you living this call today? Is the Spirit calling you to new possibilities of service and witness in the Church? Pray for guidance, and if possible discuss these new directions with a spiritual director.

2. The laying on of hands is an important symbol in our Church tradition. This gesture symbolizes the transfer of power — commissioning someone for a certain mission. Read and reflect on the following Scripture references which associate the laying on of hands with the transfer of power and the presence of the Holy Spirit.
- Acts 6:1-6
- Acts 8:14-19
- Acts 9:10-20
- Acts 19:1-7
- 1 Timothy 4:14

3. The Spirit gives different people different gifts to live the life of Christ and to build the Christian community. What gifts has the Spirit given you? How are you using these gifts? Read and reflect on the gifts listed in the following Scripture references.
- Wisdom, understanding, counsel, strength, knowledge, fear of the Lord: Isaiah 11:1-2
- Wisdom, knowledge, faith, healing, mighty deeds, prophecy, discernment of Spirits, varieties of tongues, interpretation of tongues: 1 Corinthians 22:4-11

4. How can you grow in experiencing the fruits of the Spirit in your life? Pray and reflect on this and on the following Scripture passage:

The fruit of the Spirit is love, joy, peace, patience, kindness, generosity, faithfulness, gentleness, self-control....If we live in the Spirit, let us also follow the Spirit. Let us not be conceited, provoking one another, envious of one another.

(Galatians 5:22, 25-26)

Day 7

We believe in one holy catholic and apostolic Church.
We acknowledge one baptism for the forgiveness of sins.
We look for the resurrection of the dead,
and the life of the world to come. Amen.

Prayer Suggestions: We, as the Church, are called to be "good news." Reflect on how you are "good news" to others in your daily life. Pray in thanksgiving for ways God uses you to bring Christ's love to others each day.

The saints provide us with role models of what it means to love like Christ. Read and reflect on the life of a favorite saint. Establish a trusting relationship with this saint. What qualities do you admire and seek to emulate in him or her? Ask this saint to offer you support and friendship on your spiritual journey. Establish a dialogue with him or her.

Reflect on the saintly qualities you find in family members, friends, coworkers, neighbors, and so forth. In your prayer thank God for each of these people. Reflect on how these saintly qualities strengthen you and the whole Church.

What saintly qualities do you possess? In your prayer thank God for each saintly quality that you have.

CHAPTER NINE

◆

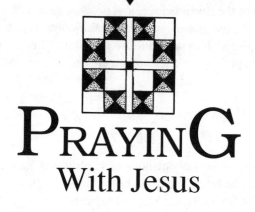

PRAYING
With Jesus

J esus experienced a loving communion with God in prayer. The gospel writers tell us that Jesus prayed at important times in his ministry. He prayed before starting his preaching ministry. "At once the Spirit drove him out into the desert, and he remained in the desert for forty days, tempted by Satan" (Mark 1:12-13). Jesus prayed before choosing the 12 apostles. "In those days he departed to the mountain to pray, and he spent the night in prayer to God" (Luke 6:12).

Jesus took time off from his busy schedule of preaching, teaching, and healing to pray. "Then he made his disciples get into the boat and precede him to the other side toward Bethsaida, while he dismissed the crowd. And when he had taken leave of them, he went off to the mountain to pray" (Mark 6:45-46).

Jesus' prayer nurtured and energized his preaching, teaching, and healing ministry.

Rising very early before dawn, he left and went off to a deserted place, where he prayed. Simon and those who were with him pursued him and on finding him said, "Everyone is looking for you." He told them, "Let us go to the nearby villages that I may preach there also. For this purpose I have come." So he went into their synagogues, preaching and driving out demons throughout the whole of Galilee.

(Mark 1:35-39)

In times of suffering and mental anguish, Jesus prayed for strength to do God's will. Sweating blood in the garden at Gethsemane, Jesus prayed in agony: "Father, if you are willing, take this cup away from me; still, not my will but yours be done" (Luke 22:42).

Nailed to the Cross, Jesus prayed for forgiveness for his executioners: "Father, forgive them, they know not what they do" (Luke 23:34). Just before his last breath, Jesus surrendered himself totally to God: "Jesus cried out in a loud voice, 'Father, into your hands I commend my spirit' " (Luke 23:46).

In the gospels Jesus provides some specific instructions on how to pray. According to Jesus' teaching, the most important issue is attitude.

When you pray, do not be like the hypocrites, who love to stand and pray in the synagogues and on street corners so that others may see them. Amen, I say to you, they have received their reward. But when you pray, go to your inner room, close the door, and pray to your Father in secret. And your Father who sees in secret will repay you.

(Matthew 6:5-6)

During the time of Jesus, the devout Jew prayed in public at set times of the day. Jesus makes the point that we should not pray in order to impress others. Rather, our prayer must be sincere. Prayer said when one is not being observed reflects the right attitude. In this saying Jesus is not referring to public common prayer in the synagogue or temple. Second, Jesus tells us that if we wish to learn to pray we need to approach God with trust and openness. "In praying, do not babble like the pagans, who think that they will be heard because of their many words. Do not be like them. Your Father knows what you need before you ask him" (Matthew 6:7-8). Jesus contrasts the Lord's Prayer with the babbling of pagan prayer. This may be a reference to the long and complicated magical formulas in which phrases were added on to make lengthy meaningless prayers. Jesus teaches us that we do not need to make a lengthy recital of our petitions since God is already aware of our needs. Third, Jesus gives clear guidelines on prayer:

This is how you are to pray:
   Our Father in heaven,
      hallowed be your name,
      your kingdom come,
      your will be done,
      on earth as in heaven.
   Give us today our daily bread;
   and forgive us our debts,
      as we forgive our debtors;
   and do not subject us to the final test,
      but deliver us from the evil one.
If you forgive others their transgressions, your heavenly Father will forgive you. But if you do not forgive others, neither will your Father forgive your transgressions.

(Matthew 6:9-15)

In the Lord's Prayer, Jesus gives us a whole new approach to prayer. Jesus spoke of God as "Abba." This was something unique. To refer to God by the familiar title "Abba" was unheard of in Jewish custom. "Abba" was, and still is in Hebrew-speaking families, an intimate name given by children to their father. When Jesus addressed his Father as "Abba," he was essentially saying "Daddy," "Dad," or "Pop." By inviting us to call God "Abba," Jesus reveals to us that we, too, have a special relationship with God. We are God's children. We, as the beloved adopted daughters and sons of Abba, are meant to participate in an intimate relationship with God. (For more information, see Joachim Jeremias, *The Central Message of the New Testament.*)

The first three petitions of the Lord's Prayer reflect the hope for the realization of the reign of God. "Hallowed be your name" is something that is happening now, but will happen in full only when the reign of God is recognized as holy by all God's people. The kingdom will come when God's will is done by all "on earth as in heaven." The reign of God will occur when God's supremacy is accepted by all of humanity.

According to some biblical scholars, the phrase, "Give us this day our daily bread," refers to the bread of the coming day. Therefore, Jesus seems to be calling on us to trust in divine providence to take care of our needs. However, K. Stendahl, a reputable Scripture scholar, thinks that this petition points to the messianic banquet because the petition is directed to the realization of the reign of God in which such daily needs no longer exist.

"Forgive us our debts" is a prayer for forgiveness that attaches to a condition. In order to be forgiven by God, the Christian must be willing to forgive the offenses of others.

In the study of theology, *eschatology* refers to doctrines which involve last or final matters like death and Final Judgment. The line of the Lord's Prayer that reads "Lead us not into temptation, but deliver us from evil" refers to the great eschatological struggle of which Matthew says that no one could survive unless it were shortened (see Matthew 24:22). This struggle is probably "the evil from which the Christian asks to be delivered in the final petition." (From *The Jerome Biblical Commentary.*)

HOW TO USE THIS METHOD

The Lord's Prayer provides Christians with rich possibilities for reflection and spiritual growth. The following prayer suggestions based on the Lord's Prayer give you an opportunity to enter into and experience God's love in a real and personal way so that you, like Jesus, may grow in a deep intimate communion with Abba.

Day 1

The Lord's Prayer

Prayer Suggestions: Say the Lord's Prayer slowly, pausing after each phrase. Allow each phrase to sink deeply into your innermost being. Be aware of any images, symbols, thoughts, or feelings that emerge. What do you feel you are learning about God by doing this? About God's presence? About you?

Read Isaiah 54:4-14 slowly several times. Imagine God saying these words to you. How do you feel after reading these words? Record your thoughts, images, insights, and feelings in your prayer journal.

The God we call "Abba," "Daddy," or "Father" loves us not because we are worthy but because we are his children. No matter how much you sin or fail, God, your loving Abba, will always love you. God loves you freely and unconditionally as the unique person you are. As you imagine, see, and feel God loving you freely and unconditionally, what are your reactions? Do you feel joy? Gratitude? Wonder? Anxiety? Peace? Share your reactions with God.

Breathe one word or line of the Lord's Prayer between inhalation and exhalation. As you do so, visualize Abba's love flowing into you more deeply with each breath. A variation is to breathe in one word of the prayer with each breath, pause during exhalation, and breathe in another word on the next inhalation.

Day 2

Our Father
who art in heaven...

Prayer Suggestions: Use the phrase "Abba, I delight in you" or "Father, I belong to you" as a form of centering prayer to remind you of God's loving presence throughout your day. Begin by reciting it when you get up and before you go to bed. Then repeat it throughout the day. Try it when driving or doing manual chores or jobs that don't require mental concentration. Both phrases contain seven syllables and can be synchronized with your breathing. Inhale on "Abba," exhale on "I delight in you." Inhale on "Daddy," exhale on "I belong to you."

Imagine God, like a loving parent, holding you close, telling you how deeply you are loved. As a child rests in the arms of Dad or Mom, relax in the embrace of your loving God.

Psalm 147 tells us why we should praise God. It calls God "good," "gracious," one who "heals the brokenhearted and binds up their wounds," and who "sustains the lowly." Share with God how you have experienced these qualities of divine love in your life. Make a "Praise God!" list or write a psalm in which you praise God for all the wonderful blessings you have received.

Go outdoors and lie on the earth or sit with your feet on the ground. Look at the sun, clouds, moon, or stars in the heavens. Allow the warmth of the sun or the beauty of the night sky embrace you. Visualize God's love streaming into your body, filling you with wonder.

Day 3

Your kingdom come...

Prayer Suggestions: Jesus has given each of us a mission.

Go into the whole world and proclaim the gospel to every creature. Whoever believes and is baptized will be saved; whoever does not believe will be condemned. These signs will accompany those who believe: in my name they will drive out demons, they will speak new languages. They will pick up serpents [with their hands], and if they drink any deadly thing, it will not harm them. They will lay hands on the sick, and they will recover.

(Mark 16:15-18)

God calls us to share our gifts with others. What specific gifts is Jesus inviting you to use in building the kingdom of God? What is your specific mission? Spend time sharing with Jesus your thoughts, feelings, and response to his invitation.

What are the fears that keep you from proclaiming God's kingdom? Where have you sought only yourself in your family, at work, in your ministry, or in your leisure time? Can you think of times that you have given yourself for the sake of God and others? Be open to any thoughts or insights concerning how you might do more in loving service of others.

Make a list of your unchristian attitudes that keep you from proclaiming the kingdom of God in your life. List the names of people who seem to practice the Christlike attitudes that bring God's kingdom alive in the world today. What do you admire most about them? Thank God for the virtues you see in them. Decide what steps you want to take in order to become more Christlike in your attitudes. Pray for the courage to take the first step.

Slowly read the following Scripture passage.

Do not seek what you are to eat and what you are to drink, and do not worry anymore. All the nations of the world seek for these things, and your Father knows that you need them. Instead, seek his kingdom, and these other things will be given you besides. Do not be afraid any longer, little flock, for your Father is pleased to give you the kingdom.

(Luke 12:29-32)

What worries preoccupy you? Do some of these sound familiar?
- What if I get in an accident?
- What if my child becomes ill?
- What if my spouse dies?
- What if I lose my job?
- What if I can't make ends meet?
- What if…?

Anxiety and worry preoccupy us and drain our energy. They prevent the Spirit of God from freeing and empowering us to live the Christian life in a vibrant and victorious way. What worries keep you from seeking first the kingdom of God in your life? Share these worries with God. Let go of them one at a time. Give each one to God. Ask God to help you set your heart on the kingdom first. Conclude your prayer by playing or singing a favorite hymn.

Day 4

Your will be done
on earth as it is in heaven.

Prayer Suggestions: We believe that Jesus came to reveal the depths of God's boundless love. God's will for you is to open yourself to the reality of this love. All your joys, sufferings, and failures are like a splendid tapestry — each thread is connected to and forms an intricate part of the whole. Look back over your life. Can you thank God for both the joyful and painful passages you experienced? Can you say to God, "For all that has been: Thanks! For all that will be: Yes!"

What changes do you need to make in your life in order to bring it more into conformity with that of God's will? What are the blockages or obstacles to doing God's will? What steps do you need to take to bring about a greater openness to God's will? Spend time discussing these questions in a loving dialogue with God.

Pray the following passage slowly.

God, my Father....When you chose to create this world, you knew the blueprint and the design of my life: the moment of my conception, the day and hour when I would be born. You saw from all eternity the color of my eyes, and you heard the sound of my voice. You knew what gifts I would have and those that I would be without. You knew also the moment and the circumstance of my dying. These choices are all a part of your will for me. I will try lovingly to build an edifice of love and praise with these materials which you have given me. What I am is your gift to me. What I become will be my gift to you.

(*The Christian Vision* by John Powell)

What reactions do you have? As you pray, do you feel afraid? Peaceful? Joyful? Hopeful? Anxious? Loved? Restless? Share your thoughts, feelings, and reactions with God. Allow God to respond to you. How do you think God feels toward you?

Think of one event that happened to you during the past day, week, or month that really touched your heart and reminded you of God's presence. What is its meaning for you? Why did it touch your heart? Thank God for it.

Think of one personal encounter in the past day, week, or month in which you experienced the God within another person touching you. Reflect on its meaning.

Think of one personal encounter in the past day, week, or month in which you experienced the God within you touching another person. Reflect on its meaning.

Do each of these experiences reflect the unveiling of God's will in your life in different ways?

Day 5

Give us this day our daily bread....

Prayer Suggestions: Spend some time in intercessory prayer — the type of prayer in which you ask God to give you joy, peace, love, or any other thing that you and others need to build God's kingdom. One way of doing this is to picture Christ holding each person and intention in his heart. As you pray, lift up the needs of the world, the nation, and the Church, as well as your personal intentions.

Plan a celebration of thanksgiving for God's gift of someone special in your life. It might be a special dinner for a spouse, family member, friend, member of your parish staff, and so forth. Compose a song, litany, or poem describing the ways this person reflects God's presence to you. Spend time together celebrating the goodness of God in one another.

Jesus gave us his own words to pray when he said, "Give us this day our daily bread." The Christ of our faith fulfills our hunger with the gifts of his body and blood. The Eucharist transforms us into new reflections of the Body of Christ. Jesus is present in the world through our presence to our sisters and brothers.

The Eucharist becomes our window on the world, our door of union with the other human beings who inhabit the earth. The Eucharist is ultimately shared prayer, the communal experience, the corporate contemplation of the entire world. He has given us bread from heaven that we might become bread for the world.

(*Gathering the Fragments: A Gospel Mosaic*
by Reverend Edward Farrell)

Do you know anyone who needs the nourishment of your loving care? How can you become bread for the world? In what ways does the Eucharist transform you into a new reflection of the Body of Christ? In what ways is the Eucharist "a door of union with other human beings who inhabit the earth"? How can you make Jesus present in the world through your presence to others? Perhaps you know someone who is sick or lonely (an elderly neighbor, a young mother, an unemployed person). Pray for this person, but also *visit* this person. If it's appropriate, pray with the person before leaving. Offer any assistance that you can give (baby-sitting, light housekeeping, shopping, bringing a care package of food). If you do not know anyone, call your local church or visit a local nursing home or hospice and ask permission to visit someone who seldom has visitors.

Slowly and sacramentally eat a piece of bread or fruit, observing its taste, texture, and fragrance. Visualize God feeding you with energy, health, and life through each bite.

Day 6

*Forgive us our sins, as we forgive
those who have sinned against us...*

In learning to forgive others we experience a deeper oneness with Jesus and with one another. We know that Jesus forgave our sins and the sins of those who have hurt us when he suffered on the Cross.

Prayer Suggestions: Imagine yourself on Calvary, walking up to the Cross and kneeling at the feet of Jesus. Imagine the person whom you need to forgive approaching Jesus on the Cross. Allow yourself to become totally involved in this scene. Remember that forgiveness is a gift from Jesus that you cannot produce by your own efforts. Allow the forgiveness of Jesus on the Cross to fill your heart and enable you to reach and forgive the person who has hurt you.

Call or write a letter of forgiveness to someone you need to forgive. Call or write a letter requesting forgiveness for the hurt and pain you have caused another. Invite the other person to celebrate your reconciliation by dining together or in some other appropriate way.

Is there anyone in your life whom you are finding difficult to love? Ask God to help you see and love this person as God sees and loves this person. Imagine that both of you go for a long walk with Jesus. On this walk share your thoughts and feelings about this relationship with Jesus. Listen as the other person shares his or her thoughts and feelings with Jesus. Listen to Jesus share his thoughts and feelings with both of you. Allow Jesus' healing love to empower you to forgive one another. Sometimes forgiveness is a process that begins with a decision to want to forgive, and it may take time for a deep healing to occur. Be patient with the process, and continue to trust that you will be able to forgive by the power of God's forgiving love within you.

If you have difficulty forgiving someone, try this suggestion. Play some classical or religious instrumental music as background for this prayer experience. Take time to relax and quiet yourself. Ask God to take from you any impediment that might block you from forgiving another. Take your time as you get in touch with any feelings that might block you, turning over each block or obstacle to God. Visualize God as a bright light radiating warmth, forgiveness, and love into your heart. Visualize the light slowly expanding, surrounding the person whom you need to forgive with forgiveness and love.

Day 7

And lead us not into temptation,
but deliver us from evil.

Prayer Suggestions: It is so easy for us to get lost, to fail, to slip into a sudden weakness. Pray that you may recognize your own emptiness and weakness. When we are empty, aware of our own sins, weaknesses, and failures, God can touch, free, deliver, heal, and fill us. In what areas of weakness and failure do you need the light of Jesus' glory to shine? Ask Jesus to shine the light of God's glory into the empty, dark areas within you.

Light a candle to represent the light of Jesus. Pray with faith that God's power may unbind and free you from the sinful tendencies that enslave or dominate your life. As you pray imagine the light of God's glory filling the dark areas within you — transforming you into a radiant reflection of God's love to others. Recite the following prayer over and over, mentioning the area(s) of weakness in which you need most to be set free. "Come, Lord Jesus, shine the light of your glory on..." (for example my pride, my stubbornness, my fears, my anger, my relationships, my sexuality...).

Jesus came into the world to free us from every form of bondage. Jesus came to free us physically, emotionally, intellectually, and spiritually. Jesus wants us to be healed and to experience the freedom that is ours through the Cross. "By his [wounds] we were healed" (Isaiah 53:5). In this prayer exercise look at a cross or crucifix (if one is not available, imagine one). What are your obstacles, areas of darkness, weakness, sin, or temptation? Bring each obstacle to the Cross of Jesus. Ask him to free and deliver you from the power of evil. Reflect on the power of Jesus' wounds to heal each area. Repeat over and over: "By your wounds I am set free" or "By your wounds I am healed."

Saint Paul wrote, "No trial has come to you but what is human. God is faithful and will not let you be tried beyond your strength;

but with the trial he will also provide a way out, so that you may be able to bear it" (1 Corinthians 10:13). In what trial, suffering, or pain do you need God's strength? How are you being challenged to trust God in your life right now? Have you experienced a greater closeness to God during dark moments of your life? In what way can your moments of suffering become gifts to others? Are you being called to be a wounded healer to someone else by sharing the depths of your wounds with someone else? (Some examples of personal "wounds" that people hesitate to share are neurosis, loss by divorce or death, drug or alcohol dependence, rejection by family or friends, having AIDS, spouse abuse, sexual dysfunction, personality disorder, and so forth.) Share your thoughts, feelings, and insights with God. Listen to God's response.

The peace that Jesus offers his followers is his own peace, which flows from his intimate communion with Abba. The peace that Jesus gives us does not leave us during difficult times of poverty, suffering, oppression, temptation, or illness. Jesus carries us, lifting us up into the arms of our Abba. There we encounter the love that surpasses all understanding, sustaining us in the midst of darkness and misunderstanding, fear and human weakness. Reflect on the times in your life in which Jesus lifted you up. Share with Jesus your thoughts and feelings about those times. Now visualize God's love going ahead of you to a future experience, filling that time with light, healing, courage, joy, peace, and love. Remember Jesus will always be there to carry you and lift you up.

Suggested Reading

Conroy, Maureen, R.S.M. *Experiencing God's Tremendous Love.* New York: Paulist Press, 1988.

De Mello, Anthony, S.J. *Sadhana: A Way to God.* St. Louis: The Institute of Jesuit Sources, 1978.

_____*One Minute Wisdom.* Garden City, New York: Doubleday & Company, Inc., 1985.

Dobson, Theodore E. *How to Pray for Spiritual Growth.* New York: Paulist Press, 1982.

Green, Thomas H. *Opening to God.* Notre Dame, Indiana: Ave Maria Press, 1977.

_____*When the Well Runs Dry.* Notre Dame, Indiana: Ave Maria Press, 1979.

Huelsman, Richard. *Pray: An Introduction to the Spiritual Life for Busy People.* New York: Paulist Press, 1976.

_____*Intimacy With Jesus: An Introduction.* New York: Paulist Press, 1982.

Linn, Matthew and others. *Prayer Course for Healing Life's Hurts.* Ramsey, New Jersey: Paulist Press, 1983.

Merton, Thomas. *Contemplative Prayer.* Garden City, New York: Doubleday & Company, 1969.

Muto, Susan Annette. *Meditation in Motion.* Garden City, New York: Doubleday & Company, 1986.

Pennington, M. Basil. *Daily We Touch Him: Practical Religious Experiences*. Garden City, New York: Doubleday & Company, 1979.

Powers, Rev. Isaias, C.P. *Quiet Places With Jesus*. Connecticut: Twenty-third Publications, 1978.

Rupp, Joyce O.S.M. *Praying Our Goodbyes*. Notre Dame, Indiana: Ave Maria Press, 1988.

Shlemon, Barbara. *Healing Prayer*. Notre Dame, Indiana: Ave Maria Press, 1976.

Wuellner, Flora Slosson. *Prayer, Stress, & Our Inner Wounds*. Nashville, Tennessee: Upper Room, 1985.

Other helpful books on prayer...

THE HEALING POWER OF PRAYER

by Bridget Meehan, SSC, D.Min.

This powerful book helps readers find comfort and healing through prayer as they attempt to deal with pain, guilt, anxiety, loneliness, and depression. It considers the potential of healing from the Church's perspective and then introduces six types of healing prayer experiences. **$2.95**

PRAYER: A Handbook for Today's Catholic

by Reverend Eamon Tobin

This handbook combines the theory and the experience of prayer to provide Catholics with a comprehensive and practical guide to improving their prayer lives. In one volume, this book considers four simple keys to successful prayer and presents more than a dozen different prayer styles along with information, techniques, and practical suggestions. **$4.95**

PRAYERS FOR MARRIED COUPLES

by Renee Bartkowski

This book contains over seventy-five brief prayers that express the hopes, the concerns, and the dreams of today's married couples. By using this book together, couples can add a new and deeper dimension to their marriage. Shared prayer can lead to a stronger union with God and into a more intimate relationship with each other. **$3.95**

LET'S PRAY (NOT JUST SAY) THE ROSARY

by Richard Rooney, SJ

After explaining what the rosary is and how to pray it, the author offers a simple meditation for each bead. Readers will find deeper meaning in this much-loved devotion as they learn to really *pray — not just say — the rosary.* **75¢**